CLEAR AND PRESENT DANGER

Clear and Present Danger

Church and State in Post-Christian America

William A. Stanmeyer

SERVANT BOOKS
Ann Arbor, Michigan

Copyright © 1983 by William A. Stanmeyer

Book design by John B. Leidy
Cover photos by John B. Leidy. Copyright © 1983 by
   Servant Publications

Available from Servant Publications, Box 8617, Ann Arbor,
   Michigan 48107

ISBN 0-89283-156-1
Printed in the United States of America

Most scripture quotations in this book are from the Revised
Standard Version, copyright 1946, 1952 © 1971, 1973 by the
Division of Christian Education of the National Council of the
Churches of Christ in the U.S.A.

1 2 3 4 5 6 7 8 9 10   86 85 84 83

Library of Congress Cataloging in Publication Data

Stanmeyer, William A., 1934-
   Clear and present danger.

   Includes bibliographical references and index.
   1. Church and state—United States—History—20th
century. 2. United States—Church history—20th
century. I. Title.
BR516.S78 1983   261.8′0973   83-12817
ISBN 0-89283-156-1 (pbk.)

To Christian church members—that they may resist the missionaries for the World in their midst . . .

To Christian citizens—that they may realize what spirit has captured the State . . .

To Christian parents—that they may repel the roaring lion that prowls the fields of education and entertainment, stalking their children . . .

To my dear wife, Judy, and to Cathy, Johnny, Tommy, Margie, and Peter—that they may take the Sword of the Spirit in the fight we cannot avoid . . .

To Our Lord Jesus Christ—who conquered these assailants on a Sunday morn, and would share the victory with us, if we but ask.

Contents

ONE

Clear and Present Danger

"You know how to interpret the appearance of the sky, but you cannot interpret the signs of the times."
—Matthew 16:3

THIS BOOK IS A MEDITATION on the present status of Christianity in America. That status, I will attempt to show, has undergone a profound change since World War II. It is a status neither comfortable nor secure, ostensibly calm and prosperous, actually tense with the prospect of impending clash and conflict. There is considerable evidence that the uneasy truce and occasional skirmish between the forces of the world and those Christians willing to battle for their faith will break out into the modern equivalent of full-scale persecution: cultural suppression leading to legal proscription. I believe that we Christians already suffer what can justly be termed covert persecution in many areas of culture, morality, and law. Unless we repent of our spiritual laziness and civic torpor, we can expect even overt persecution.

It takes some courage—or temerity—to utter such apocalyptic words. Sometime in the early 1970s, it first crossed my mind that social and political forces were massing themselves to assault the still widespread influence of Christianity in American life. I rejected my suspicions with little reflection. After all, I had been taught that the United States was a "Christian" nation, that the new pluralism which replaced the nation's former pan-Protestant Christianity boded no change for those underlying values "all Americans" hold in common. I took it for granted that a new era of toleration and brotherhood would dawn among Protestants, Catholics, Jews, and secular humanists. Moreover, as a professor of constitutional law, I was particularly aware of the Constitution's First Amendment, which expressly prohibits an "establishment of religion" and guarantees "free exercise of religion." I did feel some unease over the materialism and pragmatism that dominated the philosophical thinking, such as it was, of perhaps ninety percent of my professorial colleagues—men and women charged with forming the thinking of the lawyers, legislators, and judges who soon would be the rule-makers for us all. But my consolation was that in the future nothing would be established as our national creed. A vigilant Supreme Court would use the Bill of Rights to ensure our liberties. Christians would be treated equally with everyone else. So why be concerned?

Other Christians probably shared these half-conscious assumptions about the place of Christianity in the post-war world. The sky did not seem to contain too many thunderclouds; the wind swirled and puffed with uncertain direction and mixed purpose. The signs of the times were not so clear: many Christians believe the country is Christian; others assert that in any event Christianity has nothing to fear from the Lords Temporal, and that talk of persecution is premature and exaggerated. Moreover, many Christians believe that the advent of the Reagan Administration betokened the apparent ascendancy of religious values. The President campaigned with the support of numerous fundamentalist ministers, more than once enunciated a basically Christian approach to some key questions, emerged from the assassination attempt with a personal sense of God's providence, and has appointed to influential positions at least a few men and women sympathetic to Christian values. If there were ominous trends emerging, the election of 1980 reversed them. Some thought the wolf had been slain before it could endanger the sheepfold.

The danger of crying "Wolf!" is that one looks rather foolish if the wolf does not come immediately. The delayed danger is that people once willing to listen begin to discount repeated alarms until at last even a genuine threat will not move them. The weather forecaster whose predicted storms do not come quickly loses credibility. And if his audience changes its mind about what a "storm" or "good weather" really amounts to, even his accurate predictions may go unheeded.

For Christians in America the "signs of the times" are ominous, not the least because many Christians have lost their ability to discern them. For most of this century, the majority of Christian Americans have deemed government their friend. The power of the state seemed the quickest way to eradicate the evils of poverty and injustice. The goals of the "social gospel" coincided with the programs of the welfare state. Fundamentalists and Roman Catholics exercised their franchise by electing candidates who promised that under them the government would have "compassion" and the state would use law, coercion, and taxation to correct the wrongs caused by economic and racial inequality. Very few voices warned of the perennial heresy in such an ideology: the elusive promise of heaven-on-earth created at the hands of Almighty Man. Fewer still pointed out that the public leaders, judges, regulators, and opinion molders who ran this powerful state were themselves less and less personally animated by the same spirit of Christian charity they publicly invoked in order to justify expanding their power to remake society. Scarcely any Christians in the 1960s and early 70s saw the connection, now emerging in powerful relief like a hulking giant coming out of the mist, between using the power of government to remake society *economically* and using that same power to remake it *morally*. Yet the omnipotent state will seek to do both. Now, as moral transformation emerges as the goal of governmental coercion—or, in some cases, such as abortion, governmental abdication—some Christians discern the possibility of persecution.

Persecution in America? I realize that to use this word runs the risk of overstating the case. The word "persecution" evokes images of lions pouncing on defenseless women and children huddled together in a Roman arena, awaiting a quick and bloody martyrdom. In modern America, the anti-Christian leaders of society do not throw Christians to the lions but employ more subtle means. These means are insidious because there seems to be so much good in their agenda and they welcome Christians who join their efforts to remake society along "progressive" lines. But as this book should make clear, the hostility of the powers of this world, ancient and modern, is comparable; the rift between their vision of the good society and the Christian's vision grows wider; and the pressures on the Christian to abandon the gospel vision and substitute for it a false secularist vision are growing. Moreover, many priests, ministers, elders, and bishops have unconsciously absorbed the world's values and thus fail to perceive the conflict between secularist ideology and Christ's gospel. Neutralized by their sympathies for forces they should resist, they default through inaction. How else can one explain the virtual silence of "mainline" religions in the face of pornography so debased and so widespread that it threatens to corrupt an entire generation? How else can one explain the failure of most priests and preachers to urge prayer and repentance to avert the just wrath of an Almighty God outraged by a level of sinfulness both quantitatively and qualitatively far greater than that of ancient Babylon? Either they are blind to events around them or they have lost that inner sight, born of faith, which sees temporal actions from the viewpoint of eternity and discerns the spiritual struggle everywhere raging in the cosmos.

The chapters that follow will point out that in the watershed generation since World War II, secular humanism took an aggressive, intolerant, even imperialistic stance. Through variegated cultural and legal changes, secular humanists have modified the public order so that it no longer reinforces Christian values or supports private religious efforts to transmit traditional standards, norms, and values to one's children. Society's public policies and laws are no longer a simple extension of the basic commitments and priorities of the Christian individuals who make up that society. In field after field of human endeavor, an extraordinary transformation has taken place, as if a butterfly has reversed the process of metamorphosis and changed from a beautiful winged flutterer back to an ugly, crawling caterpillar. A society not long ago Christian is now pagan, and the change took place right before our very eyes! At the risk of some oversimplification, one could summarize the metamorphosis this way: three decades ago, the secular humanist voice was scarcely heard in public policy; two decades ago, it was one among a few; one decade ago, it became the loudest and most influential; in the decade to come, it will seek to silence all other voices. As they seek to gain control of the organs of public policy, the secular humanists will attack enclaves of Christian communal life, such as schools, hospitals, and other charitable organizations transfused with religious commitment. Their goal will be to reduce Christian influence on public morality to the most token and accidental sort.

Consider a few concrete examples. The Supreme Court has authorized de facto abortion-on-demand—the deliberate killing of innocent unborn children. For a time the Congress even funded thousands of abortions through various health care programs. When Congressman Henry Hyde attempted to bar the use of tax funds for abortions the American Civil Liberties Union argued seriously that the Congressman's amendment was unconstitutional because its sponsor was motivated by religious beliefs. The ACLU contended that to follow religious conscience or motivation in voting for legislation is to "establish religion" and thereby violate the Constitution. This position, at root, holds that Christians should have no voice, as Christians, in forming national policy. That is, American Christians should be treated like resident aliens here on a visa: tolerated as taxpayers but denied a voice in decisions on spending those taxes; permitted to worship, but denied influence on public policy. This position reverses the biblical dictum by demanding that we render to Caesar the things that are God's!

There are further examples of state encroachment on Christians. The Internal Revenue Service decided in the late 1970s that it could revoke the tax-deductible status of Christian schools that failed a contrived and irrelevant statistical test of racial mix. The National Labor Relations Board decided that it could pass judgment on the *moral* and *spiritual* qualifications of unionized teachers in Catholic schools, as if such matters were comparable to secular concerns like wages and hours. On the state level, numerous accreditation agencies have tried to outlaw private religious schools, usually the resource-poor but intellectually top-quality new evangelical schools, because they did not live up to complicated and costly "standards" of quality.

Nor has the legal pressure been confined to educational institutions. There is evidence that some medical schools will not admit applicants unless they are willing to perform abortions. If the applicant hesitates or refuses, he is judged unfit to study medicine. Some hospitals pressure staff nurses to assist in abortions. This problem has become so acute that various legislatures have considered "conscientious objection" statutes to protect resistant nurses from reprisal, whether outright dismissal, denial of promotion, or assignment to undesirable wards or shifts. Most of the medical schools and hospitals are tax supported; that is, they are arms of government, creatures of the secular state.

I do not want to make these points without qualification. To cite concrete examples as the ground for a general conclusion is to argue by induction; to draw a valid general principle out of particulars requires a representative number of individual cases whose existence, as embodiments of *this* principle, admits no other explanation than the principle itself. I realize that in each of the above cases the government authorities took actions which may well have been sincere and sometimes admitted other interpretations. In most cases—except for some heavy-handed attempts to put Christian parents in jail because their children were not in state schools—state action has been quite subtle. Nothing like lions in an arena. I realize that the state often does have, or at least could plausibly claim, an "interest" in the matter it would control or affect. I also realize that sometimes the Christian voice on these matters seems not entirely persuasive. I am aware that the very decentralization and diversity of the attacks suggest more the ordinary processes of a complicated lawmaking system than a concerted plan of some elite group bent upon "the final solution to the Christian problem." Finally, to temper Christian suspicions, I should also note that in many cases the secular humanist law and rule-makers are themselves "good men" who, in some cases, personally avow their own Christianity.

Nevertheless, whether a concerted effort or an accidental result, an ominous pattern is developing: a multifaceted campaign is mounting to remove Christian influence from society entirely—from its schools, its medical practice, its social service institutions, its laws. This book will explore the workings of the secularist agenda in the worlds of politics, the courts, the schools, and sexual mores.

A common thread links the many facets of the secularist agenda—the denial of the sacred. The secularists' preoccupation with the present and denial of spiritual value stands in sharp contrast to the Christian sense of the sacred.

Christianity is a historical religion. Jesus Christ was a historical person. The Gospels are an accurate record of events which actually happened at a certain time. Indeed, the scriptures as a whole provide the Alpha and the Omega of human history: the Creation and Fall begin the story of God's dealing with man; the Tribulation and Last Judgment end it all. From Genesis to Revelation, the Christian knows where the world came from and where it is going.

Consequently, the Christian has a sense of beginning, middle, and end; an awareness of the past as reality; a respect for past events as capable of teaching us in the present. The Christian must be prepared even to *measure* the present and the future against this past. The perfect life was Jesus Christ's, and he lived that life nearly two millenia ago. The perfect Teaching was that of Jesus Christ, and its revelation closed with the death of John the Evangelist. Anything after the apostolinc period is a variation, a development, or new embodiment—but *never an improvement*—of the life that is Jesus Christ. Therefore the Christian in the modern age must necessarily be humble, since he can have no more to give to the future than he can learn from the past. At the same time, the Christian must be critical of his own time, to the extent that he judges its teachings, theories, isms, mores, codes, practices, discipline, and enthusiasms against the Gospel. But insofar as the Christian maintains that awareness of the past as prime reality, he uses it to judge the present. Insofar as he judges the present, he sets himself over and against the world of the present. In other words, the Christian is the world's antagonist. The *agere contra*—"to act against"—in St. Ignatius Loyola's phrase is not only a rule of personal asceticism; it is an attitude toward the entire world as the Christian finds it. This had better be his stance, for whether he likes it or not, "acting against" will surely be the stance of the world toward him.

As the Western world spends its last deposit of Christian values stored up over centuries, it loses interest in a past that stressed the action of God, fixed moral principles, firm commitments, self-discipline, and interior spiritual life. Higher education exemplifies this shift from the perennial to the immediate. "Political science" in most universities is a blend of statistics on voter habits, empirical studies, and behavioral analysis—but not much about political theory, since to study Aristotle, Plato, Augustine, Aquinas, Locke, Montesquieu, and the other great theorists would suggest that the past can teach *us* something, and would distract us from important matters such as designing polls to determine whether last week's voters will change their opinion next week.

Another example is the sad state of journalism in this country. The bulk of the news pages in our newspapers and news weeklies are devoted to yesterday's scandal, today's crisis, and the continuing saga of Congress and the President and the nations of the world at loggerheads. Television news presentations are even worse: their format and substance consist of short snippets on immediate events, as if world trends needed no more attention than ordering a quickie burger at McDonald's. And television drama gives us the nadir of present-focus. The characters lock themselves into the sensual, the immediate, the pleasure and money and power of the *now*: the women with their extraordinary youth, the men with their boundless wealth, tonight's conquest their only horizon. The television set feeds us what television writers think life is all about: enjoying the present. As students of geopolitics worry about the coming Soviet political "Findlandization" of Europe, so students of national morals perceive that Hollywood's cultural "Findlandization" of America has already happened.

This cultural denial of our spiritual past and future includes what we teach and allow our children to do. Here again the secularist agenda promotes a toxic preoccupation with the present. To deal with promiscuity, the government schools teach hedonism; the message, at root, is: don't get caught, don't get sick, don't get pregnant—but go ahead and DO IT! Syndicated columnists title articles "Indecency Is Legion"; magazines such as *Newsweek* and *Families* devote cover stories to "teenage sex"; physicians attend conferences to discuss the "right" contraceptive for teenage girls. A Catholic pediatrician told me that when he stood up at one such seminar and suggested that the best contraceptive is continence, he was met with unbelieving stares. A lone voice crying in a professional wilderness, his reminder of basic biblical morality—chastity before marriage, fidelity in marriage—was rejected out of hand by educated professionals who had absorbed uncritically the "sex education" lobby's live-in-the-present standard: fornication before marriage, adultery in marriage. In perhaps the ultimate institutionalization of the present orientation, a million couples are "living together" with the understanding that either can simply walk out whenever he or she tires of the relationship and thinks "fulfillment" will be greater in a greener pasture elsewhere. Such arrangements deny the unique importance past culture saw in marriage; they deny the future—children in this world or salvation in the next.

As a corollary to its preoccupation with the present, the secularist agenda denies spiritual value. This denial affects Christian perceptions of life in a particularly pernicious way, for it amounts to denial of inner worth. Christianity teaches that the purposes of God lie within ordinary events: a sparrow does not fall without the Father's attention; one gives a cup of water to the "least" member of the human family and he does it to Jesus Christ himself; one takes up his cross daily and follows Christ through the tedium and annoyance of ordinary events and thereby merits an eternal reward "pressed down and flowing over" and unimaginable in its splendor. Jesus Christ teaches that all things have an "inner" and an "outer" dimension—a present existence locked within space and time and visible to the naked eye; and a trans-present value rising above the temporal, capturing the eternal, but visible only to the eye of faith. This teaching is an extension of the person of Jesus Christ. He tells us bluntly—extraordinary claim!—"I am the Way, the Truth, and the Life." In his own person we see a man located within space and time and visible to the naked eye, and God, the Eternal One, grasped only by the eye of faith. Jesus Christ teaches us that the world is not just what we perceive with our senses—a place where we are born, grow, and strive, and at last fall back to the dust of the earth and ultimate nothingness. Christ rejects this pagan pessimism because, simply, it is untrue. The universe, he tells us, is the expression of the Word himself: "All things were made through him" (Jn 1:3). The universe is redeemed in Christ, yet it remains the battleground of powerful spiritual forces contending for the allegiance of mankind. Some of those forces are the embodiments of malice, and this world stands under judgment for its apostasy and sin (Rv 6ff). For the Christian, therefore, reality is "sacramental": *everything* is an outward sign of an inward spiritual dimension instituted by Christ. The meaning of reality lies in this inward spiritual dimension.

The secularists deny this sacramental nature of reality. In denying the inner value of events, they deny their meaning, and thus render life meaningless. The secularists then seek value and worth and meaning in the surface of things: what pleases the eye, what soothes the ear, what beguiles the touch. They substitute an external standard of beauty, truth, and goodness for the inner norm taught in the Gospel.

This underlying shift in philosophy helps to explain the shift in the outward events: a woman's movement that honors a career in the business world more than motherhood; parents who value their retarded newborn child so meagerly that they insist the child be starved to death, as happened in 1982 in Indiana; the growth of a group called Hemlock which urges that the law recognize the "right" to suicide and provides assistance to those who would commit suicide; and avant-garde nuns who criticized Mother Teresa of India because they perceive her work with the dying as a distraction from "systemic evils" such as poverty, racism, and military weapons. The secularist sees little value in actions which do not change this world in some measurable, material way. He denies the positive spiritual value to external events. He simply does not see beyond the surface.

Our pagan culture's preoccupation with the present and denial of the inner spiritual value of external events will make its way into our laws and, like noxious fumes polluting the atmosphere, spread spiritual sickness throughout our public life as a people. In the United States the sovereign people, through a system of legislative representation, bring their ethical norms into the task of self-government. The engines of government— legislatures, courts, regulatory bodies—transmit the community's sense of right, value, and purpose. These values are increasingly secular ones. For example, it is not surprising that the proposed Revised Federal Criminal Code contains penalties from two to five times greater for producing adulterated eggs or exceeding noise emission control standards than for producing child pornography.

This book is about Christians and the public order in a post-Christian culture. It is about the secularist agenda in our laws and institutions. It will deal with some specifics of the problem—such as the secular humanist effort to use government as a tool to effect moral change, the hostility of our courts toward Christian values, and the pressures on Christian schools. Finally, it will suggest at least an outline of a political philosophy based on scripture.

I am aware that different strains of Christian thought will

deny the merits of this discussion. Some Christians have no political philosophy; intellectually they have divorced themselves from public events and are satisfied to live good private lives. Others think that the end times are upon us and that it is therefore no longer necessary to develop valid theological principles to guide practical decisions of citizenship. For still others, Christianity must adjust to progressive thinkers and find common ground with our humanist brethren in building a just social order wherein poverty, racism, and militarism are banished. I doubt that this book will please this last group because it denies their premise that secular redemption in this world is possible through human efforts. But to the first two groups, I ask a suspension of their disbelief. Assume for the sake of argument that Christians should not divorce themselves intellectually from the currents of society, or, minimally, that they cannot because society will not let them. Assume, therefore, that the Lord wants us to figure out how we got into this trouble, at least as a precondition to repentance for our part in our deception and as a basis for discerning how we might protect our children from the troubles to come. To those who believe the Second Coming of the Lord is near, I must point out that the great apostasy is part of those end times, that the advent of the Anti-Christ precedes the End, and that the scriptures tell us that we will go through "the beginnings of sorrows":

> And when he was sitting on Mount Olivet, the disciples came to him privately, saying: Tell us when shall these things be? and what shall be the sign of thy coming, and of the consummation of the world?
> And Jesus answering, said to them: Take heed that no man seduce you:
> For many will come in my name saying, I am Christ: and they will seduce many.
> And you shall hear of wars and rumors of wars. See that ye be not troubled. For these things must come to pass, but the end is not yet.
> For nation shall rise against nation, and kingdom against

kingdom; and there shall be pestilences, and famines, and earthquakes in places:

Now all these are the beginnings of sorrows. (Mt 24:3-8)

The Lord continues, saying his disciples will be delivered up to be afflicted, put to death, hated by all nations; that there will be scandals, mutual betrayals, reciprocal hatred. He says false prophets shall rise and seduce many; and the charity of many shall grow cold because of the spread of iniquity. In verse 15 he speaks of "the abomination of desolation, which was spoken of by Daniel . . . standing in the holy place," and in verse 21 he speaks of the "great tribulation":

And unless those days had been shortened, no flesh should be saved: but for the sake of the elect those shall be shortened.

Then if any man shall say to you: Lo here is Christ, or there, do not believe him.

For there shall arise false Christs and false prophets, and shall show great signs and wonders, insomuch as to deceive (if possible) even the elect.

The believer who takes these passages seriously can argue that it would make little sense for the Lord to warn us of the troubles to come before the End if we were not in the world to face them. Whether imminent or far off, the omega of human history will come only after seductive false prophets have had their opportunity to deceive all Christians; and their alluring teaching will, along with the "sorrows" of external events, be so deceptive that this era will have to be shortened by the direct intervention of God. The replacement of Christianity with secular humanism as the dominant philosophy of our country sets the stage for the deceptions the Lord warns about in these passages.

When people "discern the face of the sky" they take appropriate measures to protect themselves if a storm is nigh. They call their children home, tie down their outside movables, shutter their windows. As Christians we must "discern the signs of the times" and take appropriate measures to protect ourselves. So let us look at those signs and consider those measures.

TWO

Christians and the Political World

If you were of the world, the world would love its own; but because you are not of the world, but I chose you out of the world, therefore the world hates you. —John 15:19

I do not pray that thou shouldst take them out of the world, but that thou shouldst keep them from the evil one. —John 17:15

As thou didst send me into the world, so I have sent them into the world. —John 17:18

THE SECULAR STATE grows more hostile to Christianity. Secular power can scarcely conceal its antagonism to Christ and his Gospel as the twentieth century moves to its end. Despite the verbal/economic/military confrontation between the secular democratic states of the West and the secular Marxist states of the East, the underlying similarity of values and outlook of leadership elites in both cultures is ominous. Though stressing discipline instead of hedonism, the secularism of Communist nations resembles the "soft" secularism in the Western nations. What Lenin's heirs accomplished quickly in the nations east of Berlin, the heirs of the Fabian socialists are building gradually in the Atlantic littoral and other English-speaking countries: total exclusion of Christian influence from the world of public affairs, from political theory and practice, and at last from the lives of individual citizens.

A quick glance at some specifics will highlight this thesis. The secularization of erstwhile Christian culture manifests itself in such trends as expanding government control—a near monopoly—over schools on every level; the purging of all Christian teaching and symbols from these schools; the introduction of relativistic sex education resulting in increased promiscuity, sexual experimentation, and the consequent spiritual numbing of a sizeable body of adolescents; the enthusiasm of scientists for biological engineering, including cloning of life forms (apparently aimed at eventual duplication of human life) and the use of artificial insemination and artificial wombs; abandonment of the Hippocratic oath's prohibition of abortion and acceptance in its stead by most of the medical profession of pretended ignorance of both biological truth about the presence of human life within the womb and the ethical judgments that necessarily follow; legal changes setting the stage for euthanasia; advancement of the theory of legal positivism—law is what the state says it is and there is no "higher" law to judge it—by both national legislatures and the national courts; widespread statist anti-family policies; abdication of the state's responsibility, through the laws, to uphold a modicum of public morality and decency, through excessive toleration of pornography; the desuetude of laws designed to discourage the practice of homosexuality; and the domination over the communications media, both print and electronic, by persons who approve these trends, give favorable coverage to the "news" about them, and promote visual entertainments that embody and glorify them.

Separately, each of these occurrences may not augur significant danger for the Christian remnant. In the aggregate, however, these and other trends suggest a vast sociomoral cleavage between two "lifestyles." "And in the morning, 'It will be stormy today, for the sky is red and threatening.' You know how to interpret the signs of the times" (Mt 16:3).

The "signs of the times" point to increasing hatred by the world.

The Calculus of the World versus the Mystery of Christ

The world has its reasons to hate Christians. Christians who truly live their faith are an embarrassment to it. They threaten it. They are a witness against it. They challenge not only its discrete practices but also its overall philosophy; they challenge both its practices and its values.

Though rooted in past history, Christianity explains both the present and the future in terms of God's unswerving providence. That explanation rejects the world's assumption that man is evolving to perfection in this world. For the Christian, history follows God's purpose, which will work out whatever his creatures, like King Canute beating against the rising tide, try to do to thwart it. That purpose is to build the new man in Christ Jesus, incorporated into his mystical body in this world, redeemed through grace and called to be sons of God and heirs of the kingdom of heaven in the community of the blessed in the next world. "But to all who received him, who believed in his name, he gave power to become children of God" (Jn 1:12).

All this offends the world. To admit a Fall is to acknowledge culpability; to acknowledge fault is to concede that one is imperfect and perfection must come, if at all, from outside oneself—from Another. To accept the guidance of God's providence is to put one's destiny in the hands of Another and to give up the independence of "doing it my way." The world equates technology with wisdom and the absence of technology with ignorance. The world is bemused by the quaint idea that a Galilean carpenter who never fingered an electric typewriter or flew in a jet plane or hosted a day-time television talk show should have anything to tell *it*. But the world is not just bemused. It is also more than a little annoyed that Christianity, like the imaginary Marxist dictatorship of the proletariat, refuses to wither away in the face of all the progress that is the world's secular equivalent of redemption.

That annoyance has deep roots. The world has never been willing to grasp the mystery of Christ: "The light shines in the darkness and the darkness has not overcome it" (Jn 1:5). That mystery goes to the essence of what it means to be a human person, of the purpose of human life, and of what human fulfillment consists of. If Jesus Christ were just another great public leader, a Thomas Jefferson or Abraham Lincoln, the world could tolerate his memory because it could keep him in his place. The world is comfortable enough with an annual dinner or a school holiday in winter for Jefferson and Lincoln, for they make no demands on us today. But Jesus is *not* just a historical figure, bound to his own epoch. He declares he will be with us all days, even unto the consummation of the world, and he makes it very plain that even the talented and wealthy ones among us can do no lasting good without him: "I am the vine, you are the branches. He who abides in me, and I in him, he it is that bears much fruit, for apart from me you can do nothing" (Jn 15:5). Not only can we do *nothing* without Jesus, it is culpable for us to refuse him entrance into our lives, to prevent him from "abiding" in us: "If a man does not abide in me he is cast forth as a branch and withers; and the branches are gathered, thrown into the fire and burned" (Jn 15:6).

Thus in the world's calculus, Christ is a threat to its complacent preoccupation with self, to its pursuit of money, to its raw hedonism, its gluttony, its pride. Insofar as they abide in Christ and he in them, Christians pose the same threat. Through its critique of the world's falsity, and through the truth of life in Christ, the religion of Christianity presents the same danger. Since it cannot rebut his teaching, deny his virtue, or disprove his miracles, the world will always fall back on the only means it knows to eradicate the presence of Jesus Christ: force. Often force is applied under the guise of law. The Scribes and Pharisees were careful to maintain the appearance of legality when they browbeat Pontius Pilate into authorizing Roman collaboration in their successful effort to murder the Lord. With greater subtlety appropriate to the complexities of lawyers' minds, it will probably be the world's tactic in America for the remainder of the twentieth century. If so, Christian believers will have to give considerable thought and prayer to how to respond.

The Lord's extraordinary comments at the Last Supper are not a complete political philosophy. Rather, they suggest the believer's relationship or stance toward the world. First, the world will hate Christians because Christ has chosen them—*because* he has snatched them away from the grasp of the world. Second, Christians will not generally be taken "out" of the world, but they do have Christ's prayer that the Father will keep them from evil in the world. Third, Christians are not to be merely passively "in" the world, but are actively "sent into" the world just as the Father sent the Son. The followers of Christ have a mission—the same mission that Christ himself had.

Christian Response I: Total Withdrawal

Christians have tried to live out these principles in a bewildering and diverse range of concrete responses. In the first few centuries of the church's young existence, many Christians felt compelled to adopt a practice of total withdrawal. As the debauchery of pagan hedonism spread, the Christian communities reacted by fleeing the cities. Many fled to the deserts, adopted a rigorous life of penance, avoided worldly contact, and awaited what they thought would be the early Second Coming of Jesus Christ. The advantage of withdrawal is obvious: the stark simplicity of their surroundings insulated them from the temptations of urban luxury, and distance buffered them from Roman soldiers obeying some emperor's persecuting whim.

This response of attempted total withdrawal seems more a result of circumstance than a reflective response to the Lord's teaching. Moreover, early Christians identified with the downtrodden, people who could easily take up their worldly goods in a sack and move from place to place like nomads. One may assume, granted the fervor of most early believers, that they saw little conflict between their practice of withdrawal and the Lord's Last Supper comments about being in the world but not of it. They understood his prayer not as a direction to stay, always, physically in the worldly society of the cities, but as a command to avoid the taint of the world wherever they were. Nevertheless, whether the early Christians thought they were following the Lord's will or merely making the best of a bad political and moral situation, their actions in the early centuries of the church do not give us modern Christians clear guidance as to "the Christian way."

External pressures against the Christian life eased when Constantine introduced tolerance of Christianity as the official policy of the Empire. Yet the problem of urban corruptions remained, and an ascetic-monastic tradition sprang up to systematize ways of life that stressed imitation of the Lord's poverty and prayer. This response seemed appropriate to many Christians as the Roman Empire began to reel under the repeated blows of barbarian invasions, as its mercenary soldiers lost the will to fight the attackers and its diluted currency lost public confidence as a medium of exchange. Civilization seemed to come apart at the seams. Not surprisingly, many neophyte Christians in these years perceived God's judgments in the doleful events of the time and saw prayer and penance as the only right way to respond.

As institutional political life crumbled, the institutional church became an alternate source of stability and continuity. The arts and learning came under the patronage of the church. For a time, during the barbarian invasion and what we have come to call the Dark Ages, the primary conservators of culture were the monasteries—peaceful centers of learning, oases of civilization in a desert of barbaric confusion. They provided physical and cultural retreat for the spiritual-minded to pursue divine things, to draw strength from the fellowship of believers, and to find freedom from worldly distractions. However, only a minority of Christians adopted such a formally strict religious way of life. The vast majority lived as ordinary citizens. They owed allegiance to their overlord or leige lord, a nobleman-landowner who was in turn beholden to a higher lord and ultimately to the king. They did not feel loyalty to a nation-state. What we today consider "civic virtue" or "the obligations of citizenship" for the better part of a thousand years had only the most remote analogy in the lives of the people of the Middle Ages. Instead, Christians lived by the requirement of fealty to their lord in return for his protection; obedience in secular affairs to his will; conformity to the immemorial customs of the people; and adherence in spiritual matters to the teachings of the church.

Throughout the millenium between roughly 500 A.D. and 1500 A.D., the problem of "Christians in the world" took a form much different from today. We can draw little guidance from the monasteries or from considerations of the papacy, an institution in that period both religious and political, sometimes a noble embodiment of the highest spiritual values, sometimes an ignoble embodiment of crass secular ambitions. The question of the clash, competition, cooperation, or "separation of church and state" was rarely satisfactorily and never permanently answered in past centuries. Even had it been, that answer would probably not fit today. Moreover, whatever the proper relation between the two structural institutions, church and state, the proper role of the *individual* Christian in worldly affairs is not automatically manifest. However, that tension between church and state contains a lesson for Christians today: *there are limits to the state's power.* As Francis Schaeffer remarks:

> Paradoxical as it may seem, the church, through its frequent tussles with secular rulers over the boundary between church power and state power, had encouraged the evolution of a tradition of political theory which emphasized the principle of governmental limitations and responsibility. There was, in other words, a limit—in this case, an ecclesiastical one—on worldly power.[1]

Of the many extraordinary results of the Protestant Reformation, two are pertinent to this discussion. On the one hand, by making the king, who is a political chief of state, the head of the church, Henry VIII adopted a mirror image of the same theory of governance as animated the papacy, with the usual mirror reversal of right and left. Whereas the pope claimed his authority from religion and used it to expand into the temporal realm, the king claimed his authority from politics and used it to expand into the spiritual realm. But the result was in many ways the same: the combination of two potentially conflicting imperatives—the claims of Caesar and the claims of God. While the Latin theory of church/state always put the church "over" the state, Henry's English theory put the state "over" the church. But by giving ultimate power to one through making the other its vassal or creature, the theorist accomplished the subordination of the other. In practice, this often meant a union: unity of leadership, ultimately unity of institutional purpose. *Cujus regio, ejus religio,* freely translated as, "The regent decides the religion," became the post-Reformation hallmark of the nascent modern political order. Out of this doctrine, through a number of permutations to be sure, came the problem of "establishment of religion" with which the American Founding Fathers had to deal quite gingerly.

One of the most serious flaws in the theory is the fact that when the political leadership controls religious affairs, as did Henry and many of the kings of Spain and France in their time, the Christian witness cowers and is muted. When the church leadership controls political affairs, the temptations of greed, ambition, and venality dilute the witness of churchmen and scandalize the laity. It seems fairly clear from history that when church and state embrace, they form a union which rarely benefits the church—though it may frequently benefit the state. Still, we must not confuse "church" and "state" with *religion* and *society.* Since the Lord expressly said (Jn 17:17) that he is sending Christians into the world, he expects them—in some way or other—to influence that society into which he sent them.

A second result of the Protestant Reformation stems from the continental Lutheran stress on faith alone as the way to salvation, strongly suggesting that good works are useless if not pernicious. Most Christians accept in theory the principle that justification is by faith alone, even though there are controversies over free will, predestination, and the fate of the "justified" human soul. But the problem at hand is more political than theological. It could be argued that the stress on faith alone, coupled with emphasis on private and individual interpretation of the scriptures, set the stage for what became a political separation of Christians from the organized community. "Individualism" in modern times is part of that tradition of withdrawal from community. Furthermore, a new school of thought taught the Christian to strengthen his faith and develop his spiritual life, but not to bother himself about the good works that political, social, and economic activity enjoined. Thus, in the United States today we have a strong tradition among many Christians to treat politics as a "dirty business" best left to unsaved worldlings. This type of individualism, in its denial of any claims on Christians as members of the corporate society, resembles the individualism of the economic and social laissez-faire libertarians. Each viewpoint stresses personal and private activity and eschews involvement in group or community purposes.

The reader should not construe these reflections as criticism of either the monastic tradition or the Reformers' theology of salvation through the primacy of faith. The point is merely that modern withdrawal-from-the-world has some historical antecedents.

Christian Response II: Faith in Action

The Last Supper discourse is not the only source of Christ's teaching about the involvement of Christians in the world. We have his Sermon on the Mount, his Good Samaritan parable, and his own personal practice of feeding the hungry and curing the sick. The early church stressed evangelical poverty and community property, and the hallmark of Christian witness was charity among the brethren: "See these Christians, how they love one another!" That tradition stayed alive through the centuries. At times whole groups of men and women would undertake to serve the poor, care for the sick, console the dying.

Indeed, the famous Mother Teresa of India is a lineal descendant and modern embodiment of this Christian tradition. One might well argue that the impulse to serve one's fellow man in secular society, from the Red Cross formed in the last century, through the extensive welfare apparatus of the modern national state, draws its inspiration from the Christian insight—now widely forgotten—that individual people, no matter how old, sick, or downtrodden, are valuable in themselves because they are children of God redeemed by Christ. As a matter of fact, it is doubtful whether much sickness and suffering would be alleviated in this world had it not been for the Christian commitment to the corporal works of mercy. The ancient pagan world showed little solicitude for suffering people.

In a more general sense, many Christians today are involved in such attractive good works in the world as alleviation of poverty and redistribution of wealth. Jesus did spend a great deal of time improving the human condition. His concern for the sick was so pervasive and continuous, for example, that one can assert that one of the works of a Christian in imitating the Lord should be an effort to heal what is broken in this world. The Lord expressly taught that if we give even a cup of cold water to the least of his brethren in his name, we have done that tiny act of charity to him. Hospitals, schools, orphanages, old people's homes all are examples of the warm charity Christians have drawn from the Gospel and practice today in this world.

However, this "social gospel" approach to Christian living is not without its difficulties. It can begin to shade into busyness about secular causes and affairs similar to the enthusiasms of the modern neo-pagan. Then too, the Good Samaritan of the Gospel was not a government agency. "Christian charity"—traditionally a voluntary person-to-person effort—loses something when modern governments make it into an agency-to-constituency effort paid for with taxes. Nor does "Christian charity" automatically entail redistribution of wealth, for there is a commandment that states unequivocally, "Thou shalt not steal," and which therefore requires sound philosophical justification for taking away a portion of the fruits of the laborer's personal work through taxes and to redistribute them to someone else.

A recent variant of the social gospel is liberation theology. Popular with many Catholic priests in Latin America and Protestant clerics in the World Council of Churches, liberation theology seeks to fuse Christian teaching about God's message with revolutionary political changes. It sees Jesus as a revolutionary, the institutional churches as collaborators with the oppressive status quo, and identifies God's purposes with the political efforts of Marxist theoreticians and rural guerrillas. At its best, liberation theology makes an incisive perception of the evils of poverty imposed by the quasi-feudal ownership system. At its worst, it adopts the Marxist commitment to secular messianism—the belief that man has the ability to create paradise here on earth through violent means justified by the goal of secular redemption. A brief paragraph cannot fully develop the nuances of liberation theology or separate in detail its gold from its dross. Suffice it to say, for Christians who draw guidance from the Roman Pontiffs, that Pope John Paul II has strongly cautioned his Latin priests against substituting politics for the Gospel and has reiterated his church's condemnation of the end-justifies-the-means ethic. For Christians who draw guidance primarily from the scriptures, one may note that the Lord remarked that the poor we will *always* have with us and admonished his disciples not to fault the woman who broke the costly jar of ointment over him even though its price might have been given to the poor.

The problem with the social gospel and liberation theology lies in a proper understanding both of ends and means. The Gospels are clear: the Kingdom of Christ is "not of this world." The Kingdom Christ seeks to establish is over the hearts of men. He demands spiritual rejuvenation, insists that we be "born again of water and the Holy Spirit," makes it plain that we cannot serve both God and mammon, and tells us without equivocation that our calling is to lay up treasure in heaven. Thus the end or purpose of Christian life is the spiritual renewal, in and through Christ, of the individual soul. Though the missionary-cum-rifle might maintain his rightful priorities, more often he succcumbs to the rhetoric of revolution and the excitement of "the struggle" to the detriment of his spiritual life. Then he stops reading the scriptures meditatively, has no time for prolonged prayer, and transforms his preaching from the theme of building Christ in one's life to the theme of tearing down the corrupt social structures around him. Corrupt they indeed may be; but the means to destroy corruption must be proportionate to what replaces that corruption. One does not make fire with water. If one would replace one political structure with another, then political means are adequate; but if one would replace a political structure with a spiritual one, then only spiritual means are adequate. Insofar as the messianic revolutionary violates the teaching of scripture on godly conduct, ceases to love his enemies and pray for those that hurt him, or adopts evil means to attain good ends, to that extent he rejects the guidance of Christ and his Spirit.

Christian Response III: The Restoration of Morality

Christian involvement in political matters has taken another turn in America during the last few years. An energetic group of fundamentalist Christians, supported by a significant number of traditionalist Catholics, formed the loose-knit "Moral Majority" and developed a set of tests for political office based on a candidates' position on such matters as abortion, pornography, homosexuality, private schools, and United States policy toward the Soviet Union. This movement scandalized many members of the mainline denominations, both Protestant and Catholic. It also outraged the politically liberal, theologically secular humanist, groups such as the leadership of the American Civil Liberties Union, television producer Norman Lear, the editors of *Playboy, Penthouse,* and other such magazines. Many born-again Christians who previously had avoided politics became active. For a time the joke was that the preacher's job is to get the people saved and registered. The voter registration drives of the newly activist fundamentalist Christians seems to have paid off in the 1980 national elections, both in providing some support to President Reagan and probably decisive support to such newly elected senators as John East and Jeremiah Denton.

At first glance one might doubt whether political activism has much scriptural warrant. Yet just as the other Christians have texts and past historic practice to call upon to justify their approach to living out Christ's mandates, so also do the evangelical political activists. Christ himself said that a man should not leave his candle under a bushel but rather place it out in the open. He said Christians are to be the "light of the world." He declared that Christians are to be the salt of the earth; he asked where it would be salted if the salt itself lost its savor. While not unambiguous, the lesson from these teachings is at least this: Christians are to have some impact on public affairs.

The two great commandments are to love God and to love one's neighbor, but neither love takes place in a vacuum. Because of the nature of human beings, both must take place in concrete circumstances, within a framework of laws, inside the political organization which we call the state. Public affairs and public matters have impact, however subtle, on the Christian, influencing him toward righteous or unrighteous conduct. Federal Communications Commission rules on broadcasting affect the kinds of entertainments the Christian and his children will see. School board rules about student dress and conduct affect his children's perceptions of modesty and morality. The tax code's exactions often anger him with its compulsions to support ungodly projects.[2] Moreover, the Christian cannot keep his children in the house all day. However upright and moral his family may be, however Christlike in its practices and home life, as his children grow older they will spend more and more time in the schools, at drug stores, in front of magazine racks, and watching television. "The world" comes closer and closer. It enters the living room. It peers out of the textbook page. It slouches on the downtown streetcorner. When these trends enjoy the blessing and even promotion of the political authorities, it is not surprising that the exasperated Christian finally comes to the conclusion he must counterattack; when the law began to impose values upon the Christian that his faith could not countenance, it is not surprising that he concluded he must change the lawmakers.

Thus I believe that the Christian who doubts the wisdom of such forays into politics should not automatically attack his brother Christian for going that route. The problem is not that Christians get involved in politics, whether to promote morality or charity or "liberation." The problem is the temptation to make political success the measuring rod of Christian success— a temptation for the social gospel and liberation theology movements, and for the evangelical Protestant and traditional Catholic when they move into politics. This danger includes the possibility that one will profess to discover a scriptural basis for every political program one favors. Yet there is no automatic transfer from general religious principle to specific political prudence. For example, it is easy enough to move from the condemnation of adultery and homosexual practice in scripture to views about the role of law dealing with such sins. But law must be for the generality of men and women, and at times it may be wiser to temper the rigors of justice with the leniency of mercy. Again, it is easy enough to defend a nation's right to develop a military force in order to resist aggression; it is harder to conclude, from scripture alone, that the Panama Canal should not have been transferred to Panama. Though one should agree with the Apostle Paul that he who will not work should not eat, it is hard to see how that principle applies to *every* case of abuse in welfare, or mandates that the Christian vote for the candidate who calls for the abolition of the welfare system.

The profoundest problem, however, may be one of attitude and image rather than candidate and issue. If the Christian political activist gives the impression that he is just as interested in secular salvation as his worldly adversaries, he stands little chance of converting them and runs great risk of becoming just like them. This danger may be especially acute in the Christian who tries to make the jump from religion to politics, from scriptural reflection on general truths to the voting booth decision on specific candidates. He must first formulate a comprehensive philosophical understanding of his role in the state, the state's claims on him as citizen, the rights and responsibilities of members of temporal society, the interaction between law and morality and between these two and revealed truth. The practitioners of the social gospel of good works, the promoters of revolution as the route to "liberation," and the campaigners for Christian morality via hard-nosed electoral politics can fall into the same error: forgetting that "unless the Lord buildeth the house, they labor in vain who build it."

Toward a New Theory of Christian Polity

Early in this decade, there was great agitation throughout the land over the proper role of the religiously committed citizen in forming public policy. Here is a sample of church-state issues that are typical of the intensifying conflict we can expect for the next decade. I received a fund-raising letter from the American Civil Liberties Union which declared that "if the Moral Majority has its way, you'd better start praying," and asserted early in its text that "they want their religious doctrines enacted into law and imposed on everyone." Again, I also received a form letter from a right-to-life group urging my support of its efforts to block the Supreme Court appointment of Judge Sandra O'Conner. A Federal District Judge in Rhode Island directed public school authorities to permit a male homosexual student to take another male to the senior prom as his "date." To prevent him, as the authorities wanted to do, would be to interfere with his First Amendment "freedom of speech," because the Court felt that he would be "making a statement about his sexual preference" at the prom. About the same time, a New York Court struck down as unconstitutional that state's laws against sexual exploitation of minors, a ruling the U.S. Supreme Court would later reverse. But that same Supreme Court held by a 5 to 4 majority that posting the Ten Commandments on a wall in a public school violated the "establishment clause" of the Constitution. A year earlier, also by a 5 to 4 majority, the Court held that the "Hyde Amendment" prohibiting federal expenditures for elective abortions did not violate the Constitution. In Fairfax County, Virginia, as in many school districts throughout the country, controversy ebbs and flows over the emerging new "sex education" curriculum and how it will deal with abortion, homosexuality, prostitution, contraception, incest, and possibly other "taboo" subjects. Parents who sincerely question the benefits of exposing grade school children to such matters often are dismissed as religious fanatics seeking to impose their outdated puritanical religious views on others. In an extensive article in a leading law journal, a libertarian author writes snidely about the "narrow Catholic view" of sex and bluntly suggests that laws against pornography reflect religious bias.[3]

These items and many others one could mention illustrate the problem: political, philosophical, religious, and anti-religious trends and causes are contending for the public's allegiance. The goal of the anti-religious faction is to achieve a position from which their views will be accepted, even written into law. However simple things might have been in the "good old days" we think we remember, political, moral, and legal struggles are intensifying in the present epoch. These struggles are part of life in "the world." They impinge on the values we will transmit to our children, on the rules for public decency and religious presence, on the use of the power of government—whether school board dealing with a prom or Congress refusing to fund abortions. They shape the stance we take as a nation, in our entertainments, our education, and expenditure of our treasure. In the end they affect our response to God and his demands upon us.

The decade ahead will be a watershed for American Christians. Just as the 1960s saw a breakup of traditional self-confidence in foreign policy and the rise of the domestic student radical movement, just as the 1970s witnessed the aftermath of the earlier emotional trauma taking the form of a "Me

Generation" and intensified pursuit of hedonism, the next decade is likely to behold enormous social changes. But one may wonder how many modifications add up to distortion, how many distortions culminate in corruption, and how much corruption will be absorbed without destruction.

Many of the changes of the 1960s and 1970s affected the younger generation: "Don't trust anyone over thirty" was for a while a slogan of the times. Now that generation is itself over thirty, and it occupies an increasingly strong position to influence public policy through law. Many of the social changes which that generation participated in and now favors were profoundly unchristian and even anti-Christian in their thrust; the "liberation" of the "do-your-own-thing" generation invariably included liberation from the Ten Commandments. The raucous hedonoism of pot-smoking and wife-swapping routinely results in an animalistic mindset utterly blind to Christian values. Now a sizeable number of people, because of their technical education in the better universities, are in a position to create public acceptance for their libertine lifestyles. They are poised to go further, if only to justify themselves in their own eyes, to make their disvalues the norm by writing them—first permissively, then as a mandate—into law.

In the next decade the sociomoral issues that surfaced within the last ten to fifteen years will come to a head. The nation can swallow only so much pornography. It can commit only so many abortions. It can tolerate only so much homosexual practice. It can permit easy divorce only for so long. At some point or other either the nation will recoil from what it has been doing or it will try to "go all the way"—to erase from its laws and finally from its collective memory any vestiges of Christian perspective. I believe the "tolerance" of "diverse points of view" that receives such warm lip service from the keepers of our public conscience is a tolerance more in name than in reality. It is a patience and a prudence that calculates just how far it can go for the time being to eradicate Christian influence without causing a reaction. It is surely not a principled commitment to the right of Christians to influence public policy if they should have the votes, or to set the national agenda if they and others of traditional instincts should assemble a continuing majority.

As the civility of the present evaporates, Christians in the near future will have to have their philosophical house in order, so that they do not waste time and energy in ambivalence and ambiguity. They will have to develop a theory of Christian polity appropriate for our time. They must take the ancient traditions—the Fathers of the early church, the monasteries of the medieval period, the institutional claims and scriptural insights of the Renaissance Christian churches—and adapt them to our own period. Only then will we be prepared to deal courageously with the difficulties ahead.

One of the purposes of this book is to offer some reflections and analysis leading to a modern theory of Christian polity.

THREE

Christians and Modern Politics

We must obey God rather than men. —Acts 5:29

CHRISTIANS IN AMERICA are much agitated over the question of whether there a specifically "Christian" approach to politics. A corollary question is: Does being a Christian require specific positions on national issues? That is, is a Christian disloyal to his faith if he fails to take the "Christian" stand on certain issues? To put it negatively, is it either impossible or improper for believers to try to formulate—much less to enact into law—a "Christian" political order?

Central to the inquiry is whether private faith should have any influence on public policy, whether there are universal principles of general application to public affairs, and, if so, whether being a Christian gives a person some special ability to discover and apply them.

A further dimension to the question is this. Assuming that Christianity does have something valid to say to the political order, then Christians must decide when, if ever, their message is so closely connected with the teachings of Christianity that they claim virtually the same certainty for its political application as they would for its religious doctrine. Can a Christian tell the world, in effect, "Just as I can offer you the truth in religious matters, so also I can present at least some of the truth in political matters"?

At first glance it would appear presumptuous to make such a claim. Christianity itself is divided on some important religious matters; it would seem almost hypocritical for Christians to claim certainty in public policy when they cannot, so it seems, offer certainty in every area of religion. If they cannot agree on their faith, how can Christians urge agreement among non-Christians and Christians alike on such pragmatics as specific laws, government programs, taxes, and policies? One would think that this elemental difficulty should make priests and ministers pause before they tell their congregations that scripture or the church clearly teaches specifics on such political controversies as disarmament versus increased defense spending, or federal social program cuts versus expanding the money supply.

Still, unless one believes in a duality of truths—one private, one public, but neither interacting with or affecting the other—one must conclude that there is a core of basic Christian truths which can have practical political bearing. The Christian citizen has the responsibility to identify those truths, explicate them for his fellow believers and then, more broadly, for the nonbelievers who comprise possibly a majority of citizens. Because we are communal beings who have a social aspect to our nature, we must reject the idea that our religious commitments and positions have no communal application. We must cast off that intellectual dualism—a kind of philosophical schizophrenia—that characterized quite a few Christians in the past. They were unable, whether out of enervation or ineptitude, to bridge the gap between private faith and public policy; unable to relate revelation to reason; unable to connect central Christian teaching to the causes and campaigns of public policy.

For the Christian, there are immutable truths in this universe. These truths deal not only with private piety but also with public policy. The reason is that they are truths about the one human nature that God created and redeemed. Since politics is the work of managing the interaction of these human beings, one cannot have a valid political theory without knowing what kind of being it is which the political order contains. Only Christianity gives an adequate and true understanding of those human beings. Thus only Christianity can be an adequate basis for the political order. It follows that the Christian who denies that his faith has any application to public affairs cuts himself off from the primal source of wisdom. Like a man who does not bother to consult his map on his journey through a wilderness, the Christian who keeps his faith at home when he attempts to carry out his civic duties is one who is not really very interested in the guidance of truth.

The Path through the Wilderness

The path through the wilderness of politics shows both where one should be and where one should not be. Let us observe what Christianity says politics may *not* be. The *central* teaching of Judeo-Christian tradition, even before one gets to salvation history and the person of Jesus and the nature of grace or the Second Coming, is the "alpha" of all future theologizing: *God exists.*

> I am the Lord your God . . . You shall have no other gods before me. (Ex 20:2-3)

> In the beginning was the Word, and the Word was with God, and the Word was God. (Jn 1:1)

The corollary of the truth that God exists is that atheism is false. Every Christian says by his profession: atheism is a lie.

Since political life is the life of individuals extended into public community, it follows that the command to acknowledge that God exists must apply to the public community. God could hardly have meant to say: "You individuals in your private life must have no other gods before me; but in your social, communal, legal, and public lives you may have as many false gods as you want." Such a bizarre compromise would be to command virtue on the one hand but condone vice on the other. The only fair implication of God's word is that integral man, whether privately in isolation and in the small family community, or publicly as citizen and lawmaker for the tribe or the nation, *the whole man must have no gods other than the one true God*. Consequently God forbids man to build a society based on atheism.

This fact has practical political consequences. Perhaps the most obvious is that no Christian may be a Communist, for the undeviating practice of Communism declares atheism to be the *cornerstone* of the political order it seeks to create. Every Communist regime radically offends God; therefore efforts by Western governments to aid or bolster a Communist regime should arouse extreme suspicion among Christians. It could be justified only by honest prudential calculations showing that in the long run the atheistic regime would be weakened.

In domestic politics, there are functional atheists in leadership positions in both political parties. Such persons may give lip service to belief in God—they might not check the box labelled "atheist" in an opinion survey—but their calculus is exclusively utilitarian, their ethics relativist, and their view of life entirely divorced from Christian tradition or biblical principles. I believe Christians should be very hesitant to endorse such persons for elective office. Their atheism is no accident, no passing feeling like that of the rebellious teenager; it is a conscious choice in many cases, a decision to reject the Lord knocking at their hearts. This decision suggests an intellect darkened into levels of confusion it is possible to avoid. How can such a man or woman perceive the true good of society as a whole when he or she cannot perceive personal best interests? How can such a person stand up for unchanging moral principle in public life when his or her private life rejects the source of unchanging truth?

Granted, such uncompromising application of what scripture teaches about God's primacy in human affairs seems narrow or old-fashioned to many moderns. Granted too that when one must act and choose, in many circumstances prudence will seem to dictate a course of action different from the one that abstract principle seems to dictate. Admittedly, precision and clarity of principle sometimes blur as one moves down from the mountaintop of first principles into the plain of prudential application. But I believe that we Christians spend so much time on the plain of prudence that we frequently neglect the mountaintop of principles. We forget that principles are more important than practical judgments because prudence, being a matter of weighing and proportioning, actually cannot itself be exercised unless one knows *what* he is weighing. Only the principle can tell us what the issue is, and often the issue is the importance of the principle itself. So Christians must recall the principle that, to God, atheism is a totally unacceptable basis for organizing human affairs. Two facts follow from this principle: first, that God will not long bless such arrangements even though for a time he may tolerate them; second, that even if God withheld his judgment on the atheist regime, it would not work.

Having been softened by the rampant materialism of our era, we Christians sometimes act as if it did not matter whether God is part of the public life of a nation. Yet this proposition could be true only if it did not matter whether God is part of the private life of the individual. For there is an organic continuity between private and public lives. The public life of the nation is the private lives of its citizens in their public mode, taking on communal order through law and custom, and passed along among the generations through history. At all times the individual with his private life is the same individual who, with others and through the web of laws and social arrangements, forms the public order. To admit atheism as a formative principle of the public order—or to elect atheists to ruling positions—is, in effect, to admit atheism to one dimension of each man's private life. For the public and private dimensions are not two lives, but *two aspects of the same life*.

The Original Source of Political Disorder

Christianity teaches that the ultimate root of all evil in the world is original sin, or the Fall. Today the ultimate root of our inability to understand the evil in the world is our denial of the Fall.

Christian theology teaches that the Fall, like an enormous meteorite crashing into the sea, shook the very foundations of the deep and created shattering waves that reached out to the farthest shore. It is crucially important for Christians to understand the implications of their own theology on this point and to grasp as well how their position utterly contradicts the accepted wisdom of the secular humanists who dominate the leadership groups in Western culture in such crucial areas as journalism, the academy, the courts, and politics.

Modern secularists want to believe that man *ascended* from apes through the process of evolution. They deny that we descended from Adam and Eve. They deny that there were any such individual persons as Adam and Eve and of course they deny the Book of Genesis and its explanation for evil in the world.

The first disastrous effect of the denial of the Fall is that it puts the blame for evil and the imperfection of the world on God, not man. By denying that man's first parents brought evil into the world through their sin, a sin which is transferred by inheritance to each successive generation, the secularists excuse man from responsibility for the very real evil in the world. This denial of man's culpability places the blame on God—for there is no one else around. It also makes a mockery of Genesis 1:31, which says that after creating man "God saw everything that he had made, and behold, it was very good." Genesis teaches that man was in a state of grace and innocence, immortal, unable to suffer, in charge of creation, dominant over even the mighty beasts of the forest, possessing a magnificent intellect that grasped with ease all he needed to know, enjoying a true paradise.

The scriptures clearly place the blame for the shattering of this idyllic situation on man. Given a choice of good or evil, man chose evil. And bitter and bloody has been man's history since that fateful decision in the original paradise. He lost his special prerogatives; gone were his immortality, his easy control over nature, his infused knowledge. Gone was the placid order of nature itself. God wrote the death sentence on man's aging brow; dark clouds of ignorance gathered in his mind; an affinity for error and a love of evil developed as his passions clamored for satisfaction in reckless indifference to his spiritual welfare. Besides these horrible consequences in this world, culminating in the literal banishment of Adam and Eve from terrestrial paradise, a worse punishment followed automatically from their sin: because they had committed an infinite offense on account of the infinite dignity of the God offended, the gates of heaven were closed to them and their descendants. There would be no paradise in this world *or* in the next until the merits of a Divine Redeemer could rectify the terrible crime mankind had committed.

St. Paul makes this point perfectly clear in the epistle to the Romans:

> Therefore as sin came into the world through one man and death through sin, and so death spread to all men. . . . For if many died through one man's trespass, much more . . . the grace of that one man Jesus Christ abounded for many. . . . If, because of one man's trespass, death reigned through that one man, much more will . . . grace . . . reign in life through the one man Jesus Christ.
>
> Then as one man's trespass led to condemnation for all men, so one man's act of righteousness leads to acquittal and life for all men. For as by one man's disobedience many were made sinners, so by one man's obedience many will be made righteous. (Rom 5:12, 15, 17-19)

Following this teaching of Paul, Christianity has consistently taught that the human race collectively represents one moral person whose head, Adam, passed on the legacy of brutality, perversity, and concupiscence inherent in our race. This concept of the human family as one moral person is the basis for the theology of the advent of Christ as Redeemer. For, as the new head of the human race, intimately united to men by a true brotherhood, he passed on to us a capacity to share in his divine nature. Adam's guilt is transmitted through heredity; we are all united to him by blood lines. Similarly we cannot share in Christ's merits unless he also is our blood brother, a human being like ourselves. This he is, a man descending from the lineage of David and choosing to be born of the Virgin Mary.

Notice how the secular humanist changes all this. First, he denies that God created the universe "good"; this denial is either a denial that God exists at all, or that his creation was flawless. Either way, God is in the way and is banished. Second, he denies that man introduced evil into the world; man is inherently good, he says. To explain the obvious and pervasive fact of evil, the secularist blames *externals*—the "system" or "the ruling class" or "capitalism" or "racism" or "the welfare state" or "socialism."

By blaming externals, such as environment, the secular humanist absolves himself of any guilt. In his thinking, the evils he privately commits—and we are all sinners—have nothing to do with social or political disorder. Wars, conflict, exploitation, brutality are not expressions of God's judgment on sinful men and women. They occur because essentially good human beings have not quite found the correct formula, the right "peace plan," the perfect method of "conflict resolution," the best negotiating technique. Yet by rejecting repentance and conversion, the secularist is left with no plausible way out of our dilemma. On the private level, we have self-indulgent and hedonistic pursuit of ego as usual. In the public sphere, our political leaders grope blindly for the right external manipulation to ensure, not the "peace of Christ," but a counterfeit harmony in which governments temporarily paper over the unruly resentments and hatreds of unredeemed individuals.

By denying the Fall, the secularist denies the central point in scripture: evil exists in the world because man sinned; evil can be banished only by the coming of the sinless Redeemer. Scripture teaches that as a continuation of the curse we are under, the Redeemer himself will not restore all the consequences of original innocence until he comes again. Though redeemed, we still must work by the sweat of our brow, still suffer, still deal with the consequences of our rebellion. Indeed,

Jesus Christ teaches that patient acceptance of the will of God in these matters can help sanctify the individual soul; he also points out that worldly success—a kind of recapturing of paradise—can be spiritually dangerous. The secular humanist scoffs at these teachings. The fictional heroes of modern television dramas, for instance, in such currently hit shows as *Dynasty* and *Dallas,* are invariably embodiments of wealthy greed. The political goals of the secularists—whether "hard," as in the Soviet Union, or "soft," as in the United States—boil down to an urgent and aggressive struggle to build the earthly paradise, to banish sickness, poverty, inequality, war, and every other consequence of what the scripture teaches are results of sin. These efforts will fail because they fail to banish the sin itself.

Thus the secular humanist denial of the Fall automatically entails denial of Jesus and his mission: Jesus destroyed sin, but permitted its consequences to remain; the secularist wants to be redeemed from sin's consequences but to be permitted to continue to sin.

It naturally follows that the secular humanist will insist on a political redemption. Like the Scribes and the Pharisees of old, he wants a political kingdom; like the multitude whom Jesus fed, he wants a Messiah who will ensure comfortable well being here and now. Since authentic Christianity has always followed the Lord in rejecting such a perversion of his mission, the secularist seeks to eradicate authentic Christianity. He can do this in three ways: by force, as in the Soviet Union; by law, as increasingly in the United States; or by infiltration, a tactic used in both East and West by which the secular humanist convinces Christians that their mission is essentially political and that they must make common cause with collectivist politics in both East and West.

The denial of the Fall undergirds the secularist preference for collectivism. If man did not sin, his nature is not wounded. Lord Acton's observation that "power corrupts, and absolute power corrupts absolutely" is not a rule of human nature but at most a description of past accidental excesses. The secularist may concede that power corrupts the unenlightened, but he holds that an authoritarian central government will not be corrupted if enlightened moderns run it. Those who have the right formula, program, or Five-Year Plan will move society rapidly toward the recapture of paradise on earth. Besides, "corruption" suggests a departure from norm or nature; but since man evolved *up* from the undefined ooze, who is to say what man's "nature" really is? Who is to say our political tower shall not reach to the very heavens themselves?

Thus the logic of the denial of the Fall is especially ironic for Christians who cooperate with it. As some Christians intensify their politicization of the Gospel in frantic pursuit of an earthly paradise that scripture makes plain is beyond our reach, they cast their lot in with enemies of the Gospel. Both they and their secularist counterparts condition themselves, through their denial of man's sinfulness, to accept without resistance the scripture-predicted coming of the Antichrist, whose pseudonym is the Man of Sin!

Personal Responsibility

Another political truth implicit in Christian belief is that *man is a free and responsible moral agent.* If man's behavior were somehow conditioned by genetic code or social externals, then no just judge could blame him for the evil he commits. But the scripture teaches unequivocally that God blamed Adam and Eve for succumbing to the temptation to disobedience and punished them accordingly. This theme of personal moral responsibility begins in Genesis and continues throughout the Old Testament. The instances are too many to recount here, but the lesson recurs again and again throughout the history of the chosen people: God will bless those who are faithful to his commands and will punish those who are not. The zig-zag history of the ancient Jews, alternating between independent prosperity and conquered captivity, is a reflection, in public deeds and recorded history, of the moral choices of the people and of God's response to them. No one has ever said that God was unfair to the Israelites because "they couldn't help themselves," because they inherited a genetic propensity to idolatry, or because the pagan social environment around them so overwhelmed their consciences that they no longer could be fairly considered free moral agents. Quite the contrary: scripture makes it clear that there is absolutely no excuse for sin, whether it be Cain's murder of Abel, or the Jewish nation's infidelity to God's commands. Furthermore, the nation that has sinned remains morally free to repent and return to God's way:

> If at any time I declare concerning a nation or a kingdom, that I will pluck up and break down and destroy it, and if that nation, concerning which I have spoken, turns from its evil, I will repent of the evil that I intended to do to it. (Jer 18:7-8)

The educated groups and the leaders of the people have the capacity to freely choose or reject God's moral commands. God takes it very seriously if they abuse their freedom and fall below the standard that he sets for them:

> And now, O priests, this command is for you. If you will not listen, if you will not lay it to heart to give glory to my name, says the Lord of hosts, then I will send the curse upon you and I will curse your blessings; indeed I have already cursed them, because you do not lay it to heart. (Mal 2:1-2)

The New Testament continues this theme of personal responsibility with the clarity of lightning. "Not every one who says to me, 'Lord, Lord,' shall enter into the kingdom of heaven, but he who does the will of my Father who is in heaven. . . . Every one then who hears these words of mine and does them will be like a wise man who built his house upon the rock" (Mt 7:21, 24). Jesus teaches that men are free to "do the will of the Father" or not to do it. He says he will reward those who have done well: "For the Son of man is to come with his angels in the glory of his Father, and then he will repay every man for what he has done" (Mt 16:27). Christ not only teaches that he will reward and punish the works of human free will; he goes on to demand that we actually overcome our genetic propensities, cultural conditioning, and peer group pressures and *choose* to do and forbear deeds that the natural man would find virtually impossible:

> But I say to you . . . Love your enemies, do good to those who hate you, bless those who curse you, pray for those who abuse you. To him who strikes you on the cheek, offer the other also. (Lk 6:27-29)

It would make no sense for Jesus to tell us to love our enemies if our natural propensity to hate our enemies was so strong that we could not overcome it. There is no point in urging self-control and voluntary kindness if these virtues are impossible to attain. It is an extraordinary comment on God's view of human freedom that Jesus would teach the Israelites, heirs to the tradition of "eye for an eye" and reprisal, that they should do good to those who hated them and pray for people who mistreated them. It is a counsel of impossibility—*if* one accepts the behaviorist belief that human beings cannot really help themselves because genes or environment "make" them act as they do.

Christianity, then, insists on human free will. It insists that humans are capable of good however bad the environment, and equally capable of evil however good the environment—witness Adam and Eve! Indeed, the Christian knows that "evil" and "good" are never matters of environment, but are always matters of the inner human heart. To make a careful distinction sometimes lost on moderns, there are different kinds of evil—physical and material, moral and spiritual. For example, though poverty is a material evil (granted the premise that having a comfortable share of the world's benefits is good), poverty cannot be in itself a moral evil.

We can draw many lessons for political theory from the fact that human beings are responsible moral agents because they have wills which are free. First, it provides a test by which we can measure politicians' promises and scholars' theories. The Christian doctrine of free will tells the Christian to be skeptical of those who promise goodness through political action—whether revolution, more government programs, or budget manipulation. These things are externals and, as such, cannot "make" people be good. If the promisor really believes that his external programmatic can usher in an era of human happiness, then he equates the physical/material realm with the moral/spiritual. If he goes so far as to believe that leadership in the public worldly order can offer total social and personal fulfillment—both public prosperity and private happiness—he is denying the essential Christian teaching that externals are not *capable* of providing redemption, happiness, or even lasting psychological fulfillment. (In Robert Hugh Benson's prophetic novel, *The Lord of the World*, published at the beginning of this century, the masses and the intelligentsia accept the Antichrist because they are taken in by his plausible promises of a lasting era of peace and plenty.)

A second political implication of human moral responsibility is the priority it places on the spiritual side of man's nature. As the incisive political theorist Fr. James Schall writes,

> What is unique to Christianity in relation to politics is the grounding and justification of the absolute validity of the human person, who is finite and fallible, and the placing of ultimate happiness outside of political processes. Paradoxically, politics cannot be politics unless men first find the answer to their destiny *not* in politics.

Out of this correct insight comes a number of corollaries. Since the human person is intrinsically valuable, the structures of society should be designed to foster those elements in the person which generate that value and contribute to his ultimate transcendent destiny—namely, his intellect and will, character, and correct moral choice. To put this first corollary somewhat differently, the structures of society should not get in the way of spiritual development. The second corollary of the observation that human destiny is not in politics is that politics should not absorb or preoccupy the whole human person. This means that Christianity condemns in principle all totalitarian regimes as violative of the rights and nature of human beings. Furthermore, all democratic welfare-state regimes *tend* toward the same condemnation for the same reason, because at root they substitute a politics of envy and expropriation, in the name of "justice," for the personal prayer, repentance, and effort to carry out the will of God which are central to any authentic redemption.

A third implication of the doctrine of original sin is that it protects the Christian citizen from the mistake of believing that the correct economic plan or legal formula can somehow right the wrongs of the world. Since evil is in the heart and not primarily in external arrangements, and since human beings will have hearts with evil in them as long as they do not submit to the grace of God, it follows that whatever *public* arrangements they make, people will nonetheless have a society with evil in it. Indeed, the rulers themselves have hearts with evil in them. Even if they came up with the right plan or formula in the abstract, in application they are sure to fail. This point seems so obvious that it is hardly worth making were it not for the undoubted historical fact that during this century thousands of intelligent men and women of undoubted goodwill have adopted the Marxist faith that the right economic plan, managed by intelligent men and women of undoubted goodwill, can make the world a perfect place to live. One reads the literature of revolution going back to Marx's *Communist Manifesto* and Lenin's *State and Revolution* with dumbfounded amazement that people can seriously urge amoral and even immoral means to achieve total power, and then seriously believe that those who gained power through immoral means will suddenly become wise and moral in their exercise of it. In the "classless society," the Marxist believes, not only will the lion lie down with the lamb, but the lion of revolution will turn into the lamb of gentle administration. Such magic is the stuff of fairy tales, the *Wizard of Oz*, perhaps. In the real world, it is a pure act of secular faith.

In sum, Christianity insists, as a matter of doctrine, as a given beyond argument, that (1) God exists and that atheism cannot work as a basis for political order; (2) human beings are free and responsible moral agents; (3) manipulation of externals such as heredity and environment can never fully dispel man's potential for evil or bring happiness in this world; (4) the individual human person has transcendent value; and (5) the political order must be limited in its demands for human allegiance and in its absorbtion of human energies.

One can put these truths as a series of short normative axioms: First, men should not build a society on atheism; society should be open to, perhaps even encourage, religious influence on public affairs. Second, society should not impede or interfere with the development of individual moral character; it should promote personal accountability for moral choices. Third, society should not rely solely on public arrangements for human betterment. These are intrinsically incomplete and can never reach the essence of the problem, which is spiritual. Rather, society should tolerate human finitude and imperfection. Fourth, society should not think collectively. Rather it should strive to recognize the value of each human being, a value which comes not at the sufferance of the collectivity but from "outside," that is, from God. Fifth, government may never make a legitimate total claim on the individual. It must permit him leisure, privacy, time, and opportunity for pursuits of the spirit.

Theological Truths and Political Order

However true as abstract propositions, these statements will not cause trumpets to blare and armies to march. Though they contain explosive potential, on their face they seem bland enough, indeed so prosaic that the Christian may deem them worthless as sources of guidance for dealing with the modern democratic state. The non-Christian, if he is disinclined to philosophizing, may find them equally useless. Yet the ordinariness of these principles arises in no small measure from the depth into which they have penetrated the soul of Western man since Christ. They are part of our patrimony, and even those who have left our forefathers' house—today most of the elite leadership—still feel nostalgia for the old way of looking at things. Then too, we in the West are in the habit of regarding absolute principles as irrelevant. We try to avoid such messy confrontations as revolutionary upheavals, whether the clash of soldiers in the streets or of ideas in the mind. Rather we pride ourselves in "pluralism" and "seeing all points of view," effectively reducing objective truth to the status of subjective opinion: interesting, quaint, but lacking universal validity and binding force. We like to relegate absolute principles to the position of one more statue among many in the Greek Parthenon (Acts 17). The irrelevance of absolutes conveniently frees us for technocratic management of society. Most nations of the Western world, as far as I can see, do not guide their public affairs by conscious effort to apply absolute principle. Instead, they drift along using a calculus of utilitarian convenience and pragmatics, until someone pulls them up short with a shout that some things are right or wrong in themselves. The reaction to the Supreme Court's abortion edict was utter outrage by citizens who believe some things *are wrong in themselves* and thus beyond the power of the state to authorize. The angry response by the pro-abortion segments is to insist that "pluralism" requires that "all points of view" be granted equal validity. They are angry, of course, because they do not believe there are any absolute truths, and they resent those who do.

The principles set out in the previous section are not the only premises for politics one can draw from Christian theology, but they are some of the fundamentals. For insofar as Christianity teaches basic truth it is explaining reality. Reality is the way things actually are. To the degree that a person rejects the Christian world view, he rejects reality; his thinking abandons the way things actually are. His mind is somewhere else. If he is consistent and has the courage of his mistaken convictions, he may at last go mad, as did Nietzsche; establish a hellish police state with pogroms and Gulags, as did Stalin; or preside over the murder of millions of innocent Jews, as did Hitler. But very few people are such giants of iniquity. Most of us do evil or good on a small scale and influence the public order only by our acquiescence in other persons' wrongdoing or by supporting with our vote a person or policy that fails to comport with Christian reality and may even directly conflict with it. Later in our discussion I will attempt an application of some of these principles to specific policy debates today.

But at this point we have to let the central thesis sink in. Ideas—good or bad—have consequences. Christianity offers true ideas, good ideas. These true ideas *matter*; they make a difference. The leaders of society and its people cannot deny them with impunity. The central doctrines of Christianity—God exists, God punishes sin, man is free, the person transcends politics—are not optional or "private beliefs" which must be tolerated in a pluralist democratic society because it is difficult for government to eradicate them, but which are no more guides for conduct than the erstwhile popular belief that the earth is flat. It is impossible for Christianity to be "theologically true" and not have practical political consequences. Truth is the conformity of the mind to reality. Because his theology is true, the Christian's mind is conformed with reality in the area of that truth.

Theology does not say much about the truth of engineering principles, such as how to build a safe bridge; nor about the truth of medical principles, such as how to treat cancer or rehabilitate a heart attack victim; nor the truth of economic principles, such as how to reduce inflation. But theology does say an enormous amount about the truths that bear on living a spiritually safe life, how to rehabilitate an unrighteous heart, and how to cut one's inflated attachment to material goods. Further, a Christian cannot approach the practical affairs of political judgment with the same neutrality to these

ultimate truths as his secularist fellow citizen displays. The
Christian is *going somewhere*: to the eternal Kingdom prepared for him from the foundation of the world, opened to
him by Christ's death on the cross, made his legacy because
he is now an heir of God through the action of the Spirit.
Meanwhile, he must travel through this world, live in this
country, obey and even help devise its laws, pay taxes, and
cooperate however temporarily in the enterprise of building a
just order on earth. It is quite possible and even common for
the state, in the name of this secular order, to claim an
allegiance that is more thorough and permanent than the
Christian can permit. It is likely that the state will interpose
obstacles to the Christian's progress to the eternal Kingdom,
that it will try to distract him, make it difficult for him to
worship, frighten or cajole or trick or tempt him into collaboration with its own purposes. The state will do this out of
ignorance of Christian truth, or malice, or because the mystery of iniquity works within it. It will do it by persecution,
or it will do it by subtly creating and condoning a spiritual
environment so immoral that the Christian is choked by the
noxious fumes or comes to pursue a materialist mirage of
thirst-quenching water in the distance, an image lacking
substance, ever receding as he chases it.

The "existential" truth of the Christian principles outlined
here gives the Christian citizen a way to measure some
government policies. For example, the Christian knows, with
deference to prudential considerations, that God will punish
policies which promote sin. He knows also that God takes into
account subjective ignorance and mitigating circumstances and
that those citizens who commit evil in ignorance may be less
culpable than those who acquiesce in evil with knowledge, that
there is a difference between the sinner (whom God loves) and
the sin (which God hates). But while admonished not to judge
persons, the Christian cannot help but judge public policies;
while warned against *self*-righteousness, he cannot concern
himself about *public* righteousness.

It is possible for a nation to please God or to offend God. God deals both with individuals and with communities. In history, his treatment of the communities of Sodom, Nineveh, and the Chosen People demonstrates that he is not indifferent to public or communal righteousness or immorality. "Mankind"is not just an aggregate of isolated individuals like a bunch of waterbugs darting about the surface of a stagnant pond. If this were true, then Adam's fall would not have transmitted the inheritance of original sin to his descendants, and God would not have punished nations in history because he would have ample opportunity to punish sinful individuals in eternity. "Mankind" is a general community and each nation is a specific community. A nation can enact laws which offend God because they tolerate or even promote sin. The leaders of a nation can offend God by certain immoral decisions. The most blatant offense is to initiate an unjust war. But domestic policies can offend God as well. One is entitled to believe that governmentally required or sanctioned racial segregation offends against his command of charity; governmentally encouraged abortion, the killing of innocent children, is an outrage against the commandment Thou Shalt Not Kill; government refusal to protect basic morality by using its police and prosecutorial powers against public vice offends by encouraging the breaking of commandments and scandalizing of the Little Ones, the children.

A society as a whole can be unrighteous, though it has some righteous members in it. A country's laws and public practices can reflect atheism, encourage sin, discourage spiritual character development. If a nation refuses to recognize God's Word as the basis of its laws and practices, it says to God, in effect: "As a group we deny that you exist, or that you have any claim upon us. As a community we deny there is any difference between good and evil." God cannot be indifferent to functional atheism and to communal rejection of his Word. If Christians are God's people, they cannot be indifferent to their community's collective statement to God.

Scripture and Christian Citizenship

For guidance about their civic responsibilities, Christians have the example and teaching of Jesus and the writings and conduct of the early apostles, particularly Peter and Paul. These give us some direction, though it must be admitted that scripture's guidance on civic matters is somewhat inferential and not nearly as pointed as its teaching on matters of salvation. Jesus gave himself up to arrest by the secular powers and accepted, without resistance, unjust condemnation to torture and a horrible death; from his passivity some Christians draw the conclusion that they should be pacifists. At the same time he made the famous remark that we should "render to Caesar the things which are Caesar's and to God the things which are God's." A moment's reflection indicates that "Caesar"—the state or the nation—sometimes has the right to insist that its citizens defend the nation in a defensive war against an unjust aggressor by becoming soldiers and at times engaging in mortal combat.

In 1 Peter 2:13-14, we receive some teaching that bears on our civic responsibilities. Peter tells us: "Be subject for the Lord's sake to every human institution, whether it be to the emperor as supreme, or to governors as sent by him to punish those who do wrong and to praise those who do right." In verse 18, Peter applies this counsel of obedience to slaves: "Servants, be submissive to your masters with all respect, not only to the kind and gentle but also to the overbearing." He then makes the parallel with Christ's patient suffering. Immediately thereafter, he applies the general teaching to wives: "Likewise you wives, be submissive to your husbands, so that some, though they do not obey the word, may be won without a word by the behavior of their wives" (3:1).

Without detracting from the universality of Peter's teaching, one can note that the political culture of the time was a dictatorship. Christians and other citizens of various tribes and nations ruled by the Romans had no way to influence the decrees imposed upon them by the sometimes malevolent, sometimes benevolent, dictatorship that ruled by military occupation. It would be a mistake to believe that the *sum total* of Christian teaching on civic responsibility is to "be subject . . . to every human institution, whether it be to the emperor . . . or to governors." The counsel of submission, with nothing more, would today amount to a command to abdicate the civic duties that free and enfranchised citizens have in a democratic republic as their right and responsibility. The meaning of "submission" in our democratic context in America must include the notion of *cooperation* in the affairs of the state. What Peter was saying was: "Be a good citizen; carry out your civic responsibilities as imposed by government." Today, to be a good citizen means to become knowledgeably and responsibly involved in the myriad opportunities to influence policy that a free country permits its citizens in the enterprise of self-governance. A literal interpretation of Peter's "submission" would mean, in our context, being a "bad" citizen.

In the United States, a republic with democratic institutions, slavish passivity in the face of possible abuses of governmental authority would be the opposite of the obligations of citizenship our country imposes on enfranchised voters. In the epoch that Peter and Paul lived in, control ran in only one direction: from the emperor and his provincial governors *down* to the ordinary citizen. Civic responsibility meant obedience—period. However, in our epoch control runs in *both* directions, down from Congress, the President, and the Courts; *and* up from the people, who are expected to "petition their government for the redress of grievances," to vote, to campaign, to join political parties, to write letters to their representatives, and so on. The duty to vote, which surely is a Christian duty, is part of the broader duty to take part in public affairs. To neglect his opportunities to influence the decisions of government amounts to abdication of responsibility—hardly what Peter could have been teaching. Thus we must conclude that *the mandate Peter announces, while still applicable in its direction to obey laws and edicts already in place, does not speak to the prior question of drafting and passing laws in the first place.* One cannot submit to a law that has not yet been passed or a court decision not yet handed down. But in America we can to a degree influence whether it will be a good or evil law or decree. If the Christian fails to exercise this influence, he shows little respect for the principle of authority as shared among the governors and the governed in modern America.

Because we should obey God rather than man (Acts 5:29), the modern Christian also has to answer the question whether the state's exactions and laws are sometimes so contrary to the Word of God that he cannot cooperate with them. The early Christians faced this dilemma in one concrete form: the command by some public official, often the emperor himself, that they worship the emperor or the idols of the empire under pain of martyrdom. The choice was clear, and to their credit thousands of Christians went to death rather than deny Jesus. In our times, however, the dilemma takes more subtle forms and the consequences of refusal to submit are less drastic. For example, a Christian nurse in a state-run hospital may be told to collaborate in an abortion or a Christian public schoolteacher may be told to use sex education materials that promote immorality. The consequences of refusal will be demotion or dismissal, not death. The Christian in these circumstances must reserve for himself the right to refuse to submit to the *abuse* of lawful authority after the fact—when the only choice may be to obey or to withdraw. Before the fact, the Christian in our system has opportunities to exert influence. The nurse, with her colleagues in their union, may get the work rules of their hospital to permit personal exemption from assisting at abortions. The schoolteacher may be able to convince the school board not to adopt immoral sex education texts. But there is still the larger question of what one may or even *must* do to influence the policy of the hospital or school or state as a whole. Here the conduct of both Peter and Paul is instructive.

The Book of Acts describes a head-on clash between the demands of Caesar and the demands of God. Chapter 5 describes Peter's imprisonment for preaching Jesus, his release at the hands of an angel, and his recapture by soldiers acting at the behest of the Sanhedrin. The high priest said to Peter:

> We strictly charged you not to teach in this name, yet here you have filled Jerusalem with your teaching and you intend to bring this man's blood upon us. (Acts 5:28)

After Peter responded by witnessing for the Lord with a few more comments about the crucifixion and Jesus' role as Messiah, the elders "were enraged and wanted to kill them" (5:33). Then Gamaliel, a Pharisee of relative good sense and some moderation, reminded his colleagues that the apostles' work would collapse of its own if it were a work "of men" (Acts 5:38) but "if it is of God, you will not be able to overthrow it" (5:39). The other leaders agreed to this, had the apostles beaten, and then dismissed them with the *command* "not to speak in the name of Jesus" (5:40). But we are told two verses later that *the apostles completely disobeyed this command*: "And every day in the temple and at home they did not cease teaching and preaching Jesus as the Christ."

It is true that the apostles were dealing here with the official religious authority. But since the Sanhedrin could put them into prison and had considered stoning them, it is clear that these religious leaders were wielding (under the broader Roman control) temporal authority. Of course, the apostles would have done the same if they were facing either purely religious or purely secular authority; they would completely disobey such a command, even as the later Christians completely disobeyed the command of the emperor to worship him and the Roman gods.

Paul dealt with public authority in a different way: he claimed his civil rights. Thus in Acts 16:37-40, Paul, in response to illegal arrest, invoked his rights as a Roman citizen to be publicly released and exonerated. By insisting that the government treat him fairly according to its own laws, Paul obtained his release and thus was able to continue his preaching and teaching witness. Some time later, Paul again demanded his civil rights, at the very moment when he was about to be illegally scourged:

> The tribune commanded him to be brought into the barracks, and ordered him to be examined by scourging. . . . But when they had tied him up with the thongs, Paul said to the centurion who was standing by, "Is it lawful for you to scourge a man who is a Roman citizen, and uncondemned?" When the centurion heard that, he went to the tribune and said to him, "What are you about to do? For this man is a Roman citizen." So the tribune came and said to him, "Tell me, are you a Roman citizen?" And he said, "Yes."
>
> (Acts 22:24-27)

It is clear that Paul anticipated the reaction of the Roman guards and asserted his rights in order to buy time and get himself before the Council itself so that he could preach Jesus. One lesson of his conduct is that sometimes Christians should *not* "suffer in silence." In situations where Jesus will be witnessed to better if we assert our civil rights, we are surely free to do so. It goes without saying, of course, that Paul was responsive to the Holy Spirit; if God had revealed to him a divine purpose that he suffer the scourging, Paul would have accepted it without complaint.

The lesson should be plain enough: there is an interaction between the secular and the sacral realms. Though sometimes the Christian will do better to suffer quietly the injustice that the secular authorities may inflict upon him, at other times it may be the will of God that he stand up to the secular authorities and point out to them that they are violating their own laws and that it is unjust to impose this penalty or inflict that punishment. Even in a social order that was tightly structured from the top on down, with little or no "citizen input," it was possible for the Christian to rightly disobey a command not to witness to Christ, as Peter did; or to insist on his civil rights to prevent injustice to him and to obtain an opportunity to witness for Jesus to a higher authority, as Paul did.

It would not be wise to assume that these situations are the only ones that Christians can find themselves in. As already noted, the very premise of representative government in America is that citizens will take part in their own government. Unlike the Roman Empire, which was government by the emperor and his troops, in benevolent dictatorship over their conquered subjects, today we have, in Lincoln's famous phrase, "government by the people, of the people, and for the people."

Thus the question for the Christian, being one of the "people" and thus being one of the governors, is this: what is the obligation of a governor to the other people in the society? The governor is one with a measure of power. He can, in concert with others similarly situated, make the laws. He can help persons in need. He can reform or deform the legal system. He can help set the tone of society through its public commitments to virtue or vice. Thus the question becomes, what should be the norm of conduct of the Christian citizen-governor?

When cast in this form, the question opens an enormously wide horizon. No longer is the Christian's civic obligation seen as passive only, reactive to the rules set by others, submissive to authority "out there." Paul's rights of citizenship amounted to a number of private rights encircled by all-encompassing and virtually arbitrary public power—an oasis of individual freedom in a desert of imperial whim. Modern American Christians have comparable rights, such as those protections of fundamental human dignity summed up in the Bill of Rights of the Constitution. But one cannot stop there; at least two differences exist between Paul's epoch and our own. First, today the reach and application of the very right itself needs argument and defense. Paul could simply announce the fact of his Roman citizenship and enjoy instant and automatic protection because he had a clear and universally recognized right to a fair hearing and condemnation before punishment. Today there are many cases where a general constitutional right, such as that of free exercise of religion, is not universally recognized in its application. May Christian students in public high school use an otherwise unoccupied classroom during study period to read the Bible in voluntary groups? May Oral Roberts University Law School insist, in the face of accreditation rules to the contrary, that it can apply Christian standards for student admission and faculty recruitment? These are two cases that were argued in various courts in the years 1980 and 1981. Today the mere assertion of the right is the *beginning* of the argument, not its climax as in Paul's time. But if the Christian does not even assert the right, perhaps in the mistaken view that Jesus does not wish him to assert it, then he abdicates the protections that the laws have provided for him. Worse, he abandons these protections for others. The individual may freely renounce his rights—even as the French pacifist may surrender his freedom to the invading Nazi army in 1939—but a loss-by-default becomes precedent for other comparable cases. Other Christians who may not want to surrender face a more difficult fight against the momentum of prior decision.

The second reason our epoch is different from Paul's is that our society's rules, laws, traditions, and practices call us to partake in self-government. The structure of citizenship is decidedly *not* that we just "sit back" and "do what they tell us" until, perhaps, they tell us to directly deny Christ. That is not the way our society is organized. *Since at root power is in "the people," and we Christians are among "the people," power has been given in part to us Christians.* God himself, through indirect means, to be sure, but really and truly nonetheless, has made us co-governors of this country. That means he expects us to transmit into national, state, and local public policy the definitive Christian insights which he expects us to develop. The point is not that we might abandon the country to evil men if we do nothing politically. Rather the point is that we have been anointed, crowned, with authority, as have all other citizens, and that authority includes the obligation to exercise it with prudence and wisdom. That authority is spread throughout our system. It is not just the power, right, and duty to vote.

It is the right and duty to educate oneself carefully about the candidates and the issues, to influence the development of legislation through every means that modern communications media and customary practice have made available to citizens in general. This means that we Christians are to write to our congressmen, put letters in newspapers, create television documentaries, stage rallies, get on the staffs of elected political figures, write and publish magazines and journals. We are to do all the things necessary to educate our fellow citizens and ultimately, through them, to form public policy.

FOUR

The Courts and God

When the righteous are in authority, the people rejoice;
but when the wicked rule, the people groan.
—Proverbs 29:2

OUR SUPREME COURT, along with the lower federal courts, has been a major cause of the divorce between law and national policy on the one hand, and perennial natural truths and biblical principles on the other. Though the roots of the process of deChristianization are deep, much of it took place after the watershed years of World War II, when important moral and social issues became the domain of the courts rather than the legislatures. These issues include the role of the family in society, what laws should give the family protection, the place of religion as a wellspring of policy, and questions of public morality versus private choice in such controverted matters as abortion and pornography. The country has changed enormously in its approach to such concerns since 1945. Christians had better understand how the system of "judicial review" has contributed to these changes.

Judicial Review: Murky Origin, Uncertain Reach

"Judicial review" is the scrutiny a court gives a law to determine whether it comports with the Constitution; in the American system, the courts have the power to nullify a law. In some systems of law, a "supreme" court can declare a law "unconstitutional" and still not void it—leaving that task to the legislature. In the United States the federal courts have claimed the power to nullify statutes ever since John Marshall created the power in the 1803 case of *Marbury v. Madison*.[1] In recent years, some courts have gone even further and claimed the power to direct states to take certain positive actions, such as to impose a tax to improve schools, reduce prison inmate population, or create an expansive busing scheme.

Despite the prestige of John Marshall, the nation's most eminent chief justice, scholars disagree about whether the Founding Fathers intended the Supreme Court to have what amounts to the power of being a super-legislature.[2] In a system otherwise noted for its "checks and balances" against arbitrary government power, there are no practical checks on the Court; thus there is no ready answer to the question, *What if the Supreme Court itself violates the Constitution?* Pragmatists shrug off the question, saying that it does not matter any more whether the Founders intended the Supreme Court, like the pigs compared to the horses in Orwell's *Animal Farm,* to be "more equal" than the other branches of government. They say that we have had judicial review for a long time and, they assert, it has worked tolerably well. The Supreme Court's power to interpret the Constitution, which in practice means the power to amend the Constitution, enables the Court to keep the Constitution "abreast of social changes" as a "living document" should be.

However, the Christian student of political trends is justified in raising the principle, not confined only to the Bible but equally an expression of common sense, that "by their fruits you will know them." The fruits of unrestrained judicial review have often been bitter: heightened racial animosities due to widespread busing of school children, uncontrolled pornography, abortion on demand, and the triumph of the secular humanist ideology in the public schools. The truth of the matter is that even if one assumes the Founding Fathers did intend judicial review, *they did not intend it to take the unbridled form it now has.*[3] Nor did they intend it to drive religion out of the nation's collective life. They wanted a self-consciously limited national government composed of three *co-equal* branches. No less an authority than Thomas Jefferson, in a letter written in 1804, stated that the Constitution

> meant that its co-ordinate branches should be checks on each other. But the opinion which gives to the judges the right to decide what laws are constitutional, and what not, not only for themselves in their own sphere of action, but for the Legislature and Executive also, in their spheres, would make the judiciary a despotic branch.[4]

He returned to this theme in a letter written sixteen years later:

> You seem [to] consider the judges as the ultimate arbiters of all constitutional questions; a very dangerous doctrine indeed, and one which would place us under the despotism of an oligarchy.[5]

Alexander Hamilton, perhaps the foremost proponent of judicial review, included in his case for the practice numerous qualifiers to insure, so he claimed, that the judiciary itself would not act outside the Constitution.[6] He constructed a set of *self*-imposed limits. First, he said the Court will nullify an act of Congress only when the latter violates *specific* constitutional prohibitions—for example, when it passes a bill of attainder or an *ex post facto* law—or where it enacts laws "contrary to the manifest tenor of the Constitution." "Manifest" means clear, undisputed, obvious. Further, Hamilton said that in comparing a statute with the Constitution, the judges will void the law only "if there should happen to be an irreconcilable variance between the two." That is, there must be far more than a slight difference, for *irreconcilable* means that reasonable men, no matter how skillful, will not be able to harmonize the two. Finally, Hamilton urged that the judges "should be bound down by strict rules and precedents" so that they would know their exact duty "in every particular case that comes before them." Such strictness would not leave room to manuever, blown by the winds of ideology or popular fad. Nor would there be much room for that "creative jurisprudence" that permits a bold judge to take general words like "due process" and "equal protection" and concoct a bizarre new application.

The Judiciary and the Modern Intelligentsia

All this would be only so much scholarly theory of little importance to the average American, except that in recent years the Court has utterly abandoned Hamilton's proposed limits. In doing so, it has transformed the spiritual life of our society. In many of the landmark cases, the courts have opposed values central to the monogamous family as the basic unit of society; quite often the courts have directly or indirectly assaulted basic biblical morality. Where there has been a choice, more often than not the courts in recent years have joined the modern secularist intelligentsia in rejecting Judeo-Christian values.[7]

The "militant secularist intelligentsia" might be described as a highly verbal and technically competent class of people clustered in the major prestige universities, the social service bureaucracy, the "social-change" activists in the American Bar Association, the American Civil Liberties Union, and the social gospel wings of both the mainline Protestant and Catholic national organizations, in the leadership of the women's movement (at least as regards abortion; some are having second thoughts about pornography), and in the editorial offices of most large city newspapers. They are aided and abetted by another sub-class: television writers—both those who devise the fiction that passes for drama and those who devise the fictions that pass for analysis of the news.[8]

These persons share some important characteristics. They are generally well-educated in the sense of having spent much time in formal schooling. They are largely a-religious if not anti-religious, numbering very few in their ranks who would admit being "born-again" or Bible-believers or traditional Roman Catholics. These persons have little or no training in systematic philosophy and no deep commitment to permanent ethical principles. They are future oriented and largely disdain the past as "backward." They are gravely concerned about such worrisome statistical (but not personally experienced) problems as over-population and censorship. They assume change always means progress. They believe virtually all the world's problems are manageable, at least when wise and intelligent people like themselves are the managers. They are confident that man can create peace in this world because he yearns for it and because at root all conflicts are due to misunderstanding among people of essentially goodwill. They laugh at the notion of "sin." They are concerned about the "quality of life," which invariably means not the *moral* quality of life, but the material enjoyment of the world's benefits and pleasures with as little interference as possible from God, the teachings of the Bible, the structures of the universe, or the legal/moral demands of their fellow citizens. Cosmopolitan and sophisticated, they congregate in trendy urban centers such as New York, Washington, San Francisco, Los Angeles, and to a lesser extent in cities such as Chicago, Denver, and New Orleans. They disdain the other eighty percent of America. Their political theory may be summarized as Impatient Elitism: they doubt the utility of a democratic Republic, since "the people" and their elected representatives do not move fast enough, or do not move at all in the direction that they, the militant secularist intelligentsia, want to go. They are much more at home with elitist rule-making by courts. Thus public interest law firms, litigation, "test cases," civil rights laws, and judicial decrees are their favored vehicles for social change.

Their shared or at least preferred set of values is the institutionalization of secular humanism. Their agenda is the reorganization of political, social, legal, and moral life along the lines of a utilitarian calculus of convenience, premised on the assumption that neither God nor natural law, neither Bible nor Tradition, may make any claim on Almighty Man.

I have met many of these persons in law and higher education and public policy organizations over the last twenty years. I have worked with many of them for considerable periods of time in one or another university. I am well acquainted with some, and a few I consider to be among my friends. But though they mean well and in some cases have done good in their social crusades, to some degree (varying of course with each individual) they are doing the work of the Prince of This World. And what is disconcerting is that in most cases they do not know who is the drummer to whose tune they march.

The humanistic philosophy just described may not be as intense in the federal judiciary as among some other influential groups such as television writers and professors in the "prestige" universities. Nevertheless, the judiciary has abandoned its classic role as preserver of traditional values.[9] The reason lies partly in the judiciary's adversarial role vis-a-vis the legislature, and in its power to have the last word through judicial review of legislative actions. Now I do not say that in all cases judges are necessarily "wrong" and legislators "right." My point is simply that federal judges are insulated from popular sentiment by being appointed to office and by lifetime tenure. Judges pride themselves on their independence from the popular sentiment, custom, tradition, and feelings that the people's elected representatives draw upon to assure their constituents that the representatives are indeed fulfilling the people's wishes. A judge finds it much easier to strike down an anti-pornography law or school prayer law than a legislator finds it to vote against such laws. He can do the nullifying quickly and need not worry what the people think. A paramount example of this power is the Supreme Court's decision permitting abortion. Precisely because there was widespread lack of *popular* support for abortion-on-demand in the early 1970s—only a few states had come close to this policy, and some, such as Michigan and Nebraska, had consciously rejected it—its proponents went to the courts simply as a tactical matter. They succeeded in bypassing the popular will. The rule became: when elected legislators want to maintain traditional public morality which your group wants to change, forget electoral politics and find a sympathetic judge. This is the way school prayer, Bible reading, and even display of the Ten Commandments were removed from the public schools. It is, of course, the way obstacles to abortion were removed. The effort to overturn these rulings has, typically enough, taken the form of a struggle to persuade Congress, the *elected* branch, to pass a constitutional amendment to bypass the federal courts. This struggle is an accurate barometer of public interest in given moral issues and symbolizes the tension rending our system: the people want one policy and strive to obtain it through their elected representatives; the humanist elite wants another policy, and by and large have obtained it through unelected judges.

The problem is complicated by the fact that judges are professionally different from us ordinary folk. They are all lawyers. Lawyers go through a stylized pragmatic training that stresses the "hard-nosed," the "hired-gun" mentality. They study virtually no philosophy, history, or theology. Christian influence in law schools is conspicuous by its absence. Whatever the upright lives of individual faculty members, very few law schools stress Christian values institutionally. (To my knowledge, of the half-dozen law schools in the Washington, D.C., area, not one could claim to be Christian, though a decade ago a group of evangelical laymen struggled mightily to set one up.[10]) In law school and their early legal practice, the careerists in law absorb a steady diet of court opinions crafted usually without any Christian influence. They take on a view of the world that is instrumental, pragmatic, and result-oriented. In courses dealing with the Constitution, law students have for a generation been under the tutelage of a Supreme Court itself drifting philosophically. Then too, the most energetic group of activist lawyers promoting its version of "civil liberties" is, almost to a man, secular humanist in its collective outlook. These talented and ubiquitous litigators rarely miss an opportunity to attempt to drive Christianity into the catacombs. To cap it all off, this secularist lawyering group has no counterpart ubiquitously arguing the opposite before the courts. Thus it often wins not because of the force of its logic but because of the silence of its opponents. When federal district judges (and their influential clerks) *and* the attorneys before them litigating sociomoral issues are both members of the secularist intelligentsia, the hostility of modern judicial opinion to classical Christian values is not surprising. To paraphrase G.K. Chesterton: in public policy matters, Christianity has not been "tried and found wanting"; it has been hard put to find defenders, so it has not been tried at all.

"Higher Law" in the American System

"The law of nature and nature's God" had been part of American legal philosophy from the beginning. The belief that there is a "higher law" was well-nigh universal. For our ancestors in the nineteenth century, there were two interrelated sources of rights arrayed against the state: biblical principles and natural rights discerned by enlightened reason.[11] Thus an edict of a king or enactment of a parliament did not contain its "rightness" in itself, solely from the fact that public authority had decreed it. For to claim a law was "just" simply because it was passed would give the government *carte blanche* to do anything it wanted and would deny any basis to criticize that law. Rather, the original American theory, taken over from Britain, was that there exists a transcendent order in the universe; no law could claim our allegiance unless it conformed to it.

The plausibility of judicial review stems from this assumption that there is a "higher law" against which human laws are measured. The Colonists' complaints against King George were couched in terms of the natural rights of mankind based in nature and in scripture. The judge's role, as it gradually evolved from the time of Magna Carta (1215) and especially through Lord Coke during the reign of James I, included the power to "judge" the sovereign's decrees by the standard of eternal law. Gradually this "Higher Law" took on a customary and traditional content: the "rights of Englishmen," understood as coming from time immemorial, were the cultural embodiment of the natural rights of free men that God willed his creatures to enjoy.

Early generations of Americans saw the Constitution as an expression of basic natural rights—life, liberty, and property—and of such basic "natural" governmental principles as limited government, necessary because of the corruption of human nature which tends to abuse power. Thus judicial review, while not expressly mentioned in the Constitution, is a plausible expression of the widespread view that there are norms "in the nature of things" to measure specific statutes as to their "rightness." It is a simple step from comparing a written law to the "reasonable order of nature" to comparing it to the general order of rights and allocations of powers in a written Constitution. Thus, the process is a lineal descendant from Lord Coke's famous statement in *Dr. Bonham's Case* (1610) that "the common law will control acts of Parliament [and] adjudge them to be utterly void" when such acts are "against common right and reason."[12] If gingerly applied, the doctrine of judicial review might not cause much mischief.

The practical application took the form of denying to Congress the power to achieve some substantive results. Toward the close of the last century and well into the 1930s, the Supreme Court took the position that *there were some things Congress simply could not do* because they violated the natural order of things as telescoped into a surprisingly short and really opaque phrase, "due process of law," a phrase which, from its context in the Fifth Amendment, originally meant fair *procedure* in criminal cases. For Jefferson, Madison, Adams, and the other Founding Fathers, "due process" meant right criminal procedure as practiced in England and the colonies.[13] Due process says nothing about substantive results. It does not say, surely, that Congress may not pass a minimum wage law or that states may not outlaw abortion-on-demand.

But this is what due process came to mean after the Civil War. Influenced by general notions of "natural rights" and exhilarated by independence of institutional restraint, the Supreme

Court asserted the right to invalidate legislation which in its view interfered with the "natural right" of individuals to "liberty," including their right to contract or to dispose of their property as they wished. The practice, for instance, of nullifying laws setting minimum wages or maximum hours, perceived as violating a worker's "natural right" to market his labor, reached its rhetorical apex in the famous case of *Lochner v. New York* (1905),[14] which struck down a New York law prohibiting employment of bakers for longer than ten hours a day or sixty hours a week. The case was a classic example of the Court acting as a super-legislature using what has come to be known as "substantive due process" (an oxymoron not unlike "loud silence").

This is the device the Supreme Court now uses more in sociomoral fields such as abortion. The Court said that the state abortion law was an unreasonable, unnecessary, and arbitrary interference with the right of the individual to his personal liberty. In effect, the Court took the due process clause and cut out the very words which apply to procedure, so that the clause reads: ". . . nor shall any State deprive any person of life, liberty or property," period. The specifica of the "liberty" will be the Court's to supply. By this method an unelected Court can substitute its notion of wise policy for the desires of the elected legislatures.

The dominant belief that legislatures could not tamper with certain "natural" rights also expressed itself in Supreme Court thinking on the role of parents and the family in education. In the key case of *Pierce v. Society of Sisters and the Hill Military Academy* (1925),[15] the Court upheld parental rights to educate. The case is of great importance to Christians today because it shows the potential of the judiciary to *protect* basic values when a legislature attacks them—*assuming the judges themselves understand and embrace those values.* The modern U.S. Supreme Court continues to endorse this case.

In *Pierce,* the State of Oregon yielded to some ignoble prejudices and drew upon a Know-Nothing and Nativist tradition in attempting to close the private schools by requiring

RUSH FLIER

REQUESTED BY _Dr. McKerron_

ON _____

DATE NEEDED _____

DESTINATION:

RESERVE _Spring_

HOLD SHELF _____

DATE NOTIFIED _____

MESSAGE:

PHONE _____

NOTE _____

INITIALS:

RUSH FLIER

REQUESTED BY _____

OR _____

DATE NEEDED _____

DESTINATION:

RESERVE _____

HOLD SHELF _____

DATE NOTIFIED _____

MESSAGE:

PHONE _____

NOTE _____

INITIALS:

parents to send their children to state schools for most of the first twelve years of formal education. The Society of Sisters ran a parochial school and the Hill Academy was a non-sectarian private school. To enforce the law would have destroyed them, and most other independent schools, by depriving them of clientele. Enforcement would violate parents' right to control their children's education and, in the parochial school application, violate parental free exercise of religion. In the 1920s the Supreme Court had not yet "applied" the Bill of Rights to the states, and thus the First Amendment's free exercise of religion clause could not serve as a recourse. But in fact the result was to be the same. Given the philosophy of the times that there is a "higher law" to measure human law, the Supreme Court had an apt means by which to protect the parents from the state's usurpation of the right of conscience.

The Supreme Court unanimously struck down the Oregon law as violative of the religious liberty of the parents. Though the language of the opinion stresses property rights, the Court clearly saw the issue as a clash between two competing philosophies of parental rights. From a Christian perspective in the 1980s, this is important. For unlike the 1920s, when the state-run public schools did generally embody Christianity, today the government schools institutionally reflect secular humanism. In the 1920s a conflict between parents and state-run schools might have seemed unworthy of judicial attention because, it might be said, it was a dispute between two versions of Christianity. In the 1980s, such a clash is often between Christian and secular humanist education. Fortunately, the earlier Supreme Court treated the question as one of perennial truths applicable to *any* era. It stated that

there is no general power of the State to standardize its children by forcing them to accept instruction from public teachers only. *The child is not the mere creature of the State*; those who nurture him and direct his destiny [the parents] have the right, coupled with the high duty, to recognize and prepare him for additional obligations. (Emphasis added.)

Those "higher" obligations are the transcendent claims of conscience, Bible, church, and God. To the Court, schooling, when the parents so desire, is God's. It need not be rendered to Caesar.

Judicial Edicts without a "Higher Law"

To give the judges the last word over the legislature worked tolerably well as long as the judiciary could appeal to a consensus on higher principles. As long as "liberty of contract" occupied a preferred position in economic matters because of widespread *laissez-faire* thinking, as long as the country was broadly Christian in moral matters, the judges could argue that they were applying not their own personal biases but only "the Constitution." The difficulty is that judicial activism presupposes some universal principles. Without them it degenerates into a mere *ipse dixit*—"Do it because *I* said so!"—by the elite group that happens to wield power. "We are not final because we are infallible," Justice Jackson reportedly said a generation ago. "We are infallible because we are final." This jocular remark is half right and half wrong. The Supreme Court is final indeed, but it is not infallible. Its only claim that it is not fallible in a given case depends on the correctness of its principles. But in matters of political philosophy, how can the Court claim its principles are correct if it rejects the "higher law" theory that guided the very same Court a century ago? The answer is that it substitutes ersatz principles for real ones to create the appearance of philosophical depth. It has done this in the area of abortion.

"Ersatz principles" might be too gentle a term. Someone else might use the phrase "counterfeit principles." Another way to describe them is to say that ideology can pretend to be philosophy, in a manner reminiscent of Satan imitating an Angel of Light. *Ideology is philosophy without roots in experience or revelation.* A pure creation of the mind of man, ideology almost always contains substantial portions of untruth and sometimes is totally false. The ideology of Naziism is a case in point. So too the ideology of Marxism-Leninism, "dialectical materialism," popularly known as Communism. Since humans naturally tend to believe and want to give allegiance to some body of truths which is "higher" and therefore universal, when they abandon religious faith and the accumulated philosophic wisdom of our civilization—as have most of the intelligentsia—they often substitute something else. In our century this has often been some variant of a messianic redemption-through-politics ideology. But error can take many forms. Not surprisingly, in an affluent society enjoying high technological productivity and considerable wealth, a less political ideology intermingles with the militant one. In the Western democratic nations, it is a soft preoccupation with materialistic comforts and an aggressive, almost predatory, practice of hedonism.

This preamble should help Christians understand the modern U.S. Supreme Court in the abortion cases. Christians must recognize the ideological principles behind these cases, a task doubly important now that critics of the new political involvement by evangelicals claim the evangelicals are "imposing their religious views on the rest of us."

One can trace the new "substantive due process" *without* a higher law but *with* an ideology in the Supreme Court's invention of a "constitutional right of privacy." The Court started in *Griswold v. Connecticut* (1965),[16] reviewing a statute which provided that people may not use any drug or other article for the purpose of preventing conception and that no person may assist, abet, or counsel another to use a contraceptive. Griswold, the Executive Director of Planned Parenthood of Connecticut, and another appellant, one Dr. Buxton, gave information, instruction, and medical advice to married persons about contraception. They were convicted and fined $100 each despite their claim that the statute as applied to them violated the Fourteenth Amendment. The Supreme Court struck down the Connecticut statute. The three groups of Justices who comprised the majority symbolize the philosophical fragmentation to which the Court had come. Justice Douglas and a small plurality opined as how "specific guarantees in the Bill of Rights have penumbras, formed by emanations from those guarantees that give them life and substance," and argued that elements of the First, Third, Fourth, and Fifth Amendments deal with specifics of the new "right of privacy." Out of these written specifics he drew an *unwritten* and *general* "right of privacy," which he coupled with the extra-constitutional but time-immemorially recognized right of marriage to enable him to strike down this state law. Here constitutional exegesis resembled a poetry class working through a Shakespearean sonnet: metaphors soar and images tumble and one's fancy is not bound down to the text.

Justice Goldberg, writing for himself and two other justices, took a different tack. While "joining" in the Court's (i.e., Douglas's) opinion, he urged that the Ninth Amendment suggests "additional fundamental rights" protected from government and reserved to the states or the people, and that the decision to use contraceptives is an integral part of "the right of privacy in marriage."

A third set, Justices Harlan and White, agreed with the result but, again, for different reasons. They set forth a modern application of the "Lochner" or legal natural rights theory, applied to sociomoral matters, again with stress on privacy in marriage. From this they derived the "privacy" right, that is, personal autonomy, by which they meant freedom from governmental restraint. Since in this context government is shorthand for the community acting through its legislature to maintain public standards, these Justices were saying too that there is something so special about marriage that married couples are exempt from community standards in this case. They did not raise the question of whether contraception is wrong, right, or sometimes the one or the other. Neither did they address what one could call "the contraceptive mentality"—a desire to avoid the burdens of parenthood while still enjoying the pleasures of sex, within or outside marriage—and ask whether this might not become a danger to society or offend biblical principles. One should not fault them for not entering this inquiry. It is beyond the capability of judges to assess and, in any event, these questions are properly matters for the legislature. But one must note that the three sets of Justices who joined to strike down a law passed by a Protestant Christian legislature as an expression of an important value did so because the seven Justices decided that *other* values *not even expressed in the Constitution* took precedence.

Justices Black and Stewart wrote sharp dissents. Black observed that there is no constitutional provision forbidding any law which might abridge the privacy of individual. He cited the famous Judge Learned Hand's book, *The Bill of Rights* (1958), page 70:

> Judges are seldom content merely to annul the particular solution before them; they do not, indeed they may not, say that taking all things into consideration, the legislators' solution is too strong for the judicial stomach. On the contrary they wrap up their veto in a protective veil of adjectives such as "arbitrary," "artificial," "normal," "reasonable," "inherent," "fundamental," or "essential," whose office usually, though quite innocently, is to disguise what they are doing and impute to it a derivation far more impressive than their personal preferences, which are all that in fact lie behind the decision.[17]

Black also attacked the presumed "duty of this Court to keep the Constitution in tune with the times" instead of letting the people use the process of Amendment, which is adequate to that task. Justice Stewart thought similarly, with the additional points that although a law is silly it is not thereby unconstitutional; that the Ninth Amendment, which made clear that the federal government was to be a government of limited powers, could not be the basis for invalidating a *state* statute; and that the only truly constitutional way to take the law off the books would be for the people of Connecticut to repeal it.

Confined to its own facts, the quasi-natural-law *Griswold* case would probably not do much harm. Indeed, there was much good to be said about it (prescinding from whether federal judges should have supplanted a state legislature). The idea that marriage/family intimacy is beyond the reach of the community to inhibit is, when the case's thrust is put charitably, certainly attractive to Christians. But confining *Griswold* to its own marital facts depended on the Court's commitment to the perennial Judeo-Christian and traditional-philosophy view of marriage. It was not long before the Court showed that it had lost its philosophical bearings and had, probably by osmosis, adopted the ideology of the age.

For in *Eisenstadt v. Baird* (1972) the Court expanded the newly invented right of privacy.[18] *Griswold* had involved the *use* of contraceptives by *married* persons. *Eisenstadt* overturned a conviction under a law banning *distribution* of contraceptives to an *unmarried* person. In justifying the majority's severance of the link between privacy and marriage, Justice Brennan wrote the following extraordinary statement:

> It is true that in *Griswold* the right of privacy in question inhered in the marital relationship. Yet the marital couple is not an independent entity with a mind and heart of its own [despite the Christian view based on scripture of the couple being "two in one flesh"—W.A.S.], but an association of two individuals each with a separate intellectual and emotional make-up. If the right of privacy means anything, it is the right of the *individual,* married or single, to be free from unwarranted governmental intrusion into matters so fundamentally affecting a person as the decision whether to bear or beget a child.

In a crowning irony doubtless lost on the Court, Justice Brennan then cited as authority for this bit of ersatz philosophy *Stanley v. Georgia* (1969),[19] a pornography case wherein the Court decided that the "right of privacy" permits a homeowner to insulate what the majority euphemistically called his "library" of porn films from seizure by police searching for other illegal items. In this case, the Court decided what at root was a search-and-seizure problem as if the key was freedom of speech.

Notice how the Court sets the stage for the abortion decision. First, it invents a "right of privacy" not in the written Constitution. Second, applying the Bill of Rights to states through the Fourteenth Amendment's vague due process clause, it nullifies a state law. Third, it purports to legitimate this usurpation through universal natural principle—the "higher law" natural right of husband and wife to control their sexual activity *in marriage.* But then, fourth, it cuts the *limited* privacy right free from its moorings in higher law—marriage—and lets it float free, like an errant hot air balloon, to wander where the wind blows it. Finally, it changes the contents of the balloon by pumping in the ideology of the *Zeitgeist:* marriage is out; individual autonomy is in. A secular judge can tell us that marriage is no more than a two-person business partnership. He claims to be empowered, further, to redefine the marriage-related "right of privacy" he and six other judges had conjured up just seven years and one case earlier. It now means no more than "the right of the individual," even if "single," to be free. Moreover, the Justice begs the central question: the individual is to "be free from unwarranted governmental intrusion." But the question was: what is unwarranted and what is warranted?

One answers this question by deciding when society as a whole may have some standards of marital—or single—morality and when it may use law to discourage certain conduct. It is obvious that preventing the sale of contraceptives to *unmarried* persons, many of whom would be teenagers, does serve a public purpose. Requiring some sexual self-restraint helps avoid venereal disease and prevent pregnancy (for teenagers are notorious for inconstancy in using contraceptives). From a Christian perspective, to require a society to permit sale of contraceptives to unmarried persons shows callous disregard for chastity and the Commandment, "Thou shalt not commit adultery." But the point here is not to defend the legislature's law against contraceptives so much as to note the Court's flimsy grounds for striking it down. The Court quickly abandoned the natural law/natural rights—and Christian—assumptions about marriage in *Griswold,* and replaced them with an individualistic ideology of social laissez-faire hedonism. Their position coincided with that of the secular humanists.

The Supreme Court and Abortion

No case since *Dred Scott* (1856), which held that for constitutional purposes blacks are not full persons, has caused greater controversy than *Roe v. Wade* (1973),[20] which held that for constitutional purposes unborn humans are not full persons. The case epitomized the crisis in the federal system: seven judges struck down abortion control laws in all fifty states, an extraordinary nationalization of power in a government meant to be decentralized and local. Because the Court failed to offer a persuasive rationale for its decision, the "consent of the governed" was nonexistent. By hiding behind contrived skepticism about when human life begins, the Supreme Court majority seriously compromised the Court's intellectual integrity.

In this most controversial of all political/moral issues, the Christian must be careful to have his facts straight and his theories defensible. Even those who are adamantly pro-abortion almost always give at least lip service to the Commandment that "Thou shalt not kill" an innocent human being. Consequently, the argument has focused on whether the unborn child is a human being or, in the Court's reformulation, is a "person" in the constitutional sense. The Court noted that the defenders of the traditional view

outline at length and in detail the well-known facts of fetal development. If this suggestion of personhood is established, the appellant's case, of course, collapses, for the fetus' right to life is then guaranteed specifically by the Amendment.

It seems there are three primary sources for the position that the unborn fetus is a human person: (1) scripture, (2) history and philosophy, and (3) modern medical science. Many Christians use only the first source; they cite Psalm 139:15:

> My frame was not hidden from thee,
>> intricately wrought in the depths of the earth

and verse 16:

> Thy eyes beheld my unformed substance;
>> in thy book were written, every one of them
>> the days that were formed for me

along with Jeremiah 1:5:

> Before I formed you in the womb I knew you,
>> and before you were born I consecrated you.

Christians cite the obvious implications of Luke 1:41, that the unborn human person of John the Baptist "leapt in the womb" of Elizabeth at the appearance of the nearby person of the unborn Savior, Jesus.

I believe Christians should also utilize history and philosophy for their position. Long ago the Hippocratic Oath expressly prohibited procuring an abortion; the early church condemned the practice; the Middle Age church theologians condemned it as well, with the qualifications that the fetus had to be known to be alive and, they believed, that "ensoulment" did not take place until well after conception. The common law of England condemned abortion of a "quickened" fetus, the movement of the unborn child being the only evidence, in the days of rudimentary medicine, that the woman was still pregnant with a living child that could be killed. The law also always permitted the unborn child of a father who dies before the child's birth to inherit the father's property. In modern times, tort law permits the unborn child to recover damages after birth for injuries sustained before birth. These provisions demonstrate conclusively that in such practical fields the common sense of the law is that a person exists before his or her physical birth, for the *right* to inherit or to sue for injuries does not hang somewhere in space, but rather can exist only in a person. Only persons have rights; if the unborn child were not a person, he could not enter court as a plaintiff.

Yet the third source—modern medical science—is probably the best starting point. Law must deal with facts; ethics guides and structures the law; God's Word clarifies ethics. We must go from scientific fact to ethics to law. For unless we can start with objective data that any reasonable person can accept, we must start with subjective perceptions that the public as a whole, no matter how reasonable, will not agree upon. Though many will not accept the scripture, everyone should accept the doctor's stethescope and sonic scanners, which prove that the unborn child has a separate heartbeat; the doctor's electrocephlegram, which demonstrates brain waves; and other tests, including actual photos, which show that the unborn child as early as twelve weeks has its own independent blood circulatory system, its own blood type, digestive capability, organs, its own eyes and ears and mouth and hands and even its own fingerprints.[21] Indeed, it was the American Medical Association, beginning around 1857, armed with the new science of fetology made possible by the microscope, that began the campaign to convince state legislatures to outlaw abortions. The doctors' reason was that "quickening" and "viability" are *extrinsics* unrelated to the intrinsic nature of the little being in the womb, a being which they realized began its existence at conception and went through no significant *qualitative* changes till birth. By the 1970s these facts were so well known in medical circles that no one seriously contested them. Planned Parenthood itself, today so militantly pro-abortion, in the early 1960s argued a moral case for contraception as opposed to abortion, pointing out that preventing conception was preferable to killing a child already conceived.[22] And a couple of years before the Court's 1973 abortion decision, an editorialist in the *California Medical Journal* urged permissive abortion, but candidly admitting that the pro-abortion movement had resorted to euphemisms because the "old Judeo-Christian ethic" still resisted the new ethic of convenience. The editorialist explained the abortion movement's refusal to call a spade a spade as

> a curious avoidance of the scientific fact, which everyone really knows, that human life begins at conception and is lineal, whether intra- or extra-uterine, until death.[23]

This being the state of medical knowledge, one would think that the Supreme Court would examine it. One would expect that the Court would at least cite numerous "minority" views, doctors perhaps, who disagreed that life begins at conception and claimed that human life begins at birth, or at "viability" or "quickening," or who claimed that science did not know when life began. On the other hand, the Court might have admitted the medical facts that the unborn child at twelve weeks is not *qualitatively* different than the unborn child at eight-and-a-half months, but bluntly adopt the "new ethics" and declare that biology and ethics are forever sundered because it, the Court, had decreed so.

But the Court is silent about scientific fact. It cites no endocrinologist, obstetrician, or fetologist. Though it mentions Hippocrates, Aristotle, philosophers of the Middle Ages and Renaissance, and the Catholic Church in the nineteenth century, these citations are no more than the incendiary sorties of an arsonist in a field of straw men. They are as relevant to modern medicine as the views of ancient and medieval slave-owners would be relevant to modern policy on slavery.

Then the Court plays with the word "person." It decides that "person" never appears in the Constitution with a meaning that could include unborn persons—as if one goes to a dictionary to decide whether someone is human! The irony is shattering. When holding that the "right of privacy" was a constitutional right, the Court was not deterred by the fact that the word "privacy" does not even appear in the text of the Constitution. But here, straining to rebut the critics of its narrow meaning of "person," the Court refuses to give that word the natural and universal meaning both common sense and medical science have given it for over a century. On the one hand, it can read a vague word—"privacy"—into the constitutional text though it does *not* appear there; on the other hand it can reject the clear application of a word that *does* appear.

Although the question is absolutely crucial, the Supreme Court says, "We need not resolve the difficult question of when life begins." It justifies this skepticism by alluding to a plurality of viewpoints, "a wide divergence of thinking" on the issue. It goes so far as to illustrate this claim by an outrageous statement: "There has always been strong support for the view that life does not begin until live birth." When a person living in the 1970s and 1980s reads such a preposterous remark, he is prompted to recall that there has always been support for the view that the earth is flat! Obviously, if Justice Blackmun means what his words appear to mean on their face—that the "thing in the woman's womb" *is not physically alive*—every gynecologist in the country would laugh him out of his hospital. But if he means something other than what his words clearly say, we have a mind-boggling attempt to befog with words what is clear in fact. What the overall context suggests he is obscurely saying is that "meaningful life," "life in the whole sense," does not begin until birth.

Whatever his basic thought, the Justice declares that "we do not agree that, by adopting one theory of life, Texas may override the rights of the pregnant woman . . ." although, he declares in the same paragraph, the state "has still another important and legitimate interest in protecting the potentiality of human life." Then, with scarcely any explanation, he opines as how the state's "compelling" legal and moral claim to regulate abortion for the "preservation and protection of maternal health" comes into existence out of nothing, as it were, at "approximately the end of the first trimester," the first three months. The only reason for this sudden discovery of the power to do something, however feeble, to regulate abortion is the irrelevant assertion that "until the end of the first trimester mortality in abortion is less than mortality in normal childbirth"! But for the first three months, public morality, the community, the legislature, may do *nothing* to "interfere" with the doctor/patient decision that the child in the patient's womb may be killed. During the next three months—the "second trimester"—the Justices will permit regulation that furthers the woman's hygiene and the doctor's efficiency, but will permit nothing that stops the woman from killing her offspring. Finally, after "viability" during the "third trimester," because the Court finds that "the fetus presumably has the capability of meaningful life outside the mother's womb," Texas and the other states "may go so far as to proscribe abortion . . . except when it is necessary to preserve the life or health of the mother."

But the Court backs down from even this limited restriction in the companion case of *Doe v. Bolton* (1973),[24] declaring that the physician's "best clinical judgment . . . may be exercised in light of *all* factors—physical, emotional, psychological, familial, and the woman's age—relevant to the well-being of the patient." Thus the third-trimester "health of the mother" limit becomes a rubber band stretched to cover any convenience, from pique at one's husband to continuance of a professional career to even escape from morning-sickness. "The Constitution" requires abortion-on-demand.

The two dissenters, Justices White and Rehnquist, pointed out the flaws in the majority's reasoning. Justice White noted that the majority's position amounted to saying that

> During the period prior to the time the fetus becomes viable, the Constitution . . . values convenience, whim or caprice of the putative mother more than the life or potential life of the fetus; the Constitution, therefore, guarantees the right to an abortion as against any state law or policy seeking to protect the fetus from an abortion not prompted by more compelling reasons of the mother.

Justice White dissented, because he could

> find nothing in the language or history of the Constitution to support the Court's judgment. The Court simply fashions and announces a new constitutional right for pregnant mothers, and, with scarcely any reason or authority for its action, invests that right with sufficient substance to override most existing state abortion statutes . . . [This is] an exercise of raw judicial power. . . .
>
> The Court apparently values the convenience of the pregnant mother more than the continued existence and development of the life or potential life that she carries.

Justice Rehnquist first observed that this case is a strange use of the notion of "privacy," unless it is no more than a claim for a certain kind of "liberty," but he pointed out that liberty is "not guaranteed absolutely against deprivation, but only against deprivation without due process of law." Further,

> the conscious weighing of competing factors which the Court's opinion apparently substitutes for the established test [which would uphold state legislation if it had a rational relation to a valid state objective] is far more appropriate to a legislative judgment than to a judicial one.

He then shows the similarity between *Roe* and the oft-condemned *Lochner* case, and reminds the majority that the "test" of an alleged "substantive liberty" was whether it was "fundamental," that is, "rooted in the traditions and conscience of our people." But the "fact that a majority of the States, reflecting after all the majority sentiment in those States, have had restrictions on abortions for at least a century is strong indication . . . that the asserted right to an abortion is not 'so rooted in the traditions and conscience of our people as to be ranked as fundamental.' "

Despite these two Justices' good sense, the Christian can only shudder at the decision. Its philosophy is pure and simple positivism: the belief that law is no more than the will of the Sovereign and "rights" no more than a concession by the Sovereign—or federal government—made for reasons of convenience, perhaps, but with no basis in the natural order or the will of God. Positivism holds that there is no "higher law"; consequently, whatever the government declares is the law is "good," simply because the government so decreed. Morality is no more than legality. It does not exist outside or "above" the law. Thus the lawgiver is a rule unto himself. No wonder Justice White called this case an exercise of "raw judicial power."

The Supreme Court adopted positivism in *Roe*. It adopts positivsm in ethics, for it presumes to decree that there is no connection between the immorality of abortion in the last two trimesters—there is no honest doubt in anyone's mind that a twelve- to fourteen-week-old fetus is physically a human being—and the law's obligation to control such a blatant form of immorality as willfully killing innocent human beings. It adopts positivism in jurisprudence, for it presumes that a court can strike down the ethical/legal policy set up by the people's elected representatives in all fifty states. This decision even puts the Court in the position of challenging the ancient principle that there are some limits on what Caesar may claim because some things belong to God. While pretending that it did not know whether the unborn child is a human person, the Court actually denied the Judeo-Christian conviction that every physically human being has intrinsic, God-given value.[25] Thus, clothed in a feigned skepticism about the beginning of life, and in an etymological charade about the use of the word "person" in the Constitution, the Court's opinion denied modern fetology's century-old discovery, as the *California Medical Journal* put it in 1970, that "life begins at conception and is continuous, whether intra- or extra-uterine, until death." Instead, the majority decreed that *the right to life exists not in the intrinsic nature of the human being but only in the gracious condescension of the national state*; it does not exist in reality but only in the subjective goodwill of the government. Thus the government can take it away at will.

Justice Blackmun hinted as to when the government would withdraw its subjective goodwill: when a utilitarian calculus of convenience made it expedient. Utilitarianism is the social ethic popular since at least the time of David Hume (eighteenth century) and John Stuart Mill (nineteenth century), which held that the test of "good" is not anything intrinsic but is "the greatest good of the greatest number" calculated largely in terms of pleasure and pain. Thus, early in his opinion Justice Blackmun issued a disclaimer as to how "sensitive and emotional" is the difficult problem of abortion and added,

> In addition, population growth, pollution, poverty and racial overtones tend to complicate and not simplify the problem.

He returned to this social calculus at the end of his opinion:

> This holding, we feel, is consistent with the relative weights of the respective interests involved . . . and with the demands of the profound problems of the present day.

The majority of the Supreme Court decided that such quantitative and social evils as overpopulation—elsewhere in the world, for the United States is definitely *not* overpopulated, compared with such prosperous European countries as Holland and Switzerland—and pollution and poverty have a bearing on the qualitative right of the unborn child to live. To put it another way, these quantitative judgments reduce the qualitative level of value in the unborn child. It is as if the Court said: "If the country were under-populated and we need settlers for the Far West, or if, like Russia in the 1930s, we anticipate a war and want soldiers to fight for the Motherland, then abortion would be less of a 'problem' and the individual states could more justly limit it. Perhaps then we would find that the unborn did have a 'right to life.'" Surely to reduce moral judgments about who shall live and who shall die to considerations of general population size, air and water quality, or substandard income among a statistical aggregate is the crassest of utilitarianism.

Here is the secular humanist vision of Almighty Man, eating the forbidden fruit of egotistical rejection of any Rulemaker outside himself; man building his tower to the heavens with a base spreading antiseptically from sea to shining sea; man pursuing personal convenience and economic advantage; doctors and mothers "free" to follow the spirit of the World, regardless of the teachings of scripture, history, philosophy, or even modern science.

FIVE

Church and State: The Struggle for the Schools

Train up a child in the way he should go,
and when he is old, he will not depart from it.
—Proverbs 22:6

Congress shall make no law respecting an establishment of
religion, or prohibiting the free exercise thereof . . .
—First Amendment, U.S. Constitution

ON A CHRISTIAN BROADCASTING Network television program in March, 1980, Reverend Pat Robertson asked his audience: "Does the U.S. Constitution require 'separation of Church and State?' " The audience expressed both Yes and No answers. He then inquired, "Does the Constitution even *say* anything at all about 'separation of Church and State?' " Again, mixed responses.

The correct answer to both questions is no.

What the Founding Fathers Meant

What the Founders *said* is clear from the text of the First Amendment: Congress may not set up a national church, nor may it pass federal laws against free exercise of religion. What the Founding Fathers *meant* we must glean from their own writings, the practices they tolerated or encouraged, and the meaning of the words they used at the time they used them. We do not have to resort to solving verbal puzzles about the word "respecting" or engage in cryptography to interpret the "an" used where we might have used "the."

As is well known, the Colonists had endured religious persecution. Dissenters often had to give their allegiance to an official or "established" church in return for removal of civil penalties. In some cases a person could not vote or hold colonial office if he did not swear allegiance to the "official" religion. The "established" church claimed special privileges: for example, it was entitled to a share of tax revenues to maintain its properties and often to pay the ministers' salaries. The citizen who dissented was compelled to trade away some of the benefits of citizenship in order to be faithful to his religion. This system of special preference for one religion and proportionate civil penalties for members of all others continued even after the American War of Independence, for states like Massachusetts and Connecticut kept their "established" churches into the 1800s.

Resentful of this atmosphere of religious intolerance and civil oppression, the Founding Fathers determined that the new national government would not create the same set of burdens, on a far grander and more dangerous scale, as still beset the citizens of some of the new states. In a system in which the national government had only *delegated* powers, they gave it no power over religion; and to make the point clear, the first section of the Bill of Rights expressly deprives *Congress* from passing any law that might establish organized religion. In those days "religion" meant the creed, code, and liturgical cult of the structured churches (the Church of England, Congregational, Roman Catholic, etc.), unlike our epoch when for some people "religion" means an ethical system or a vague sentiment of attention to the divine. But though the Fathers did intend to keep the institutional churches and the national government "separate," they certainly did not intend to prevent religion from having influence on society.

What the Founders did not delegate to the national government they reserved to the people and the states. This allocation of power reflected their commitment to the tradition of local control in such important matters as religion. It was natural that the First Amendment has a glaring omission: the first clause *could* have said—but does *not* say—"Neither the Congress *nor the States* shall make any law respecting an establishment of religion . . ." At the time the Constitution was adopted, New Hampshire, Connecticut, New Jersey, Georgia, North and South Carolina had religious establishments; Pennsylvania and South Carolina imposed a belief in heaven and hell; and different other sets of states variously required assent to the doctrine of the Trinity, insisted on Protestantism, or required assent to the divine inspiration of the Bible. Today, with a clearer understanding of the rights of private conscience, we realize that such arrangements violated an enlightened theory of the proper role of the State; but the point here is that they did not violate the Constitution our Founding Fathers adopted.[1]

One school of historians argues that the Free Exercise of Religion Clause is central to the Amendment and that the No Establishment Clause is ancillary; the former is the end, the latter the means.[2] They argue that the purpose of prohibiting establishment is to foster free exercise; this leaves more room for individual conscience and finesses the factionalism that invariably arises among contending groups seeking exclusive recognition by government. Whether one accepts this view or not, he is still left with grammatically coordinate statements suggesting equality of importance.[3] Indeed, Thomas Jefferson made this point clear when he wrote:

I consider the government of the United States interdicted by the Constitution from intermeddling with religious institutions, their doctrines, discipline, or exercises. This results not only from the provision that no law shall be made respecting the establishment or free exercise of religion, but from that also which reserves to the States the powers not delegated to the United States. Certainly, no power to prescribe any religious exercise, or to assume authority in religious discipline, has been delegated to the General Government. *It must then rest with the States* [emphasis added].[4]

History bears out Jefferson's view. Between 1876 and 1930, nineteen separate amendment provisions were introduced without success in Congress with the goal of making the religious provision of the First Amendment binding on the states,[5] efforts which demonstrate conclusively that no one thought, till recently under the Supreme Court's mistaken view of history, that the First Amendment already did apply, of its own force, to the states.

But through a series of Supreme Court decisions well known to students of constitutional law, in the period 1930 to the present, especially since 1947, the Court amended the Constitution, without saying so, to "apply" the religion clauses to the states. It also expanded the meaning of "no establishment" far beyond the Founders' purpose. They had intended to prevent the national government from setting up an official Church; the modern Court set out to prevent state governments from providing even indirect and non-preferential aid to religion.[6] The Founders had no difficulty with providing tax money to support chaplains in the armed forces and missionaries to the Indians; the Founders left "official" Churches to the states to create or dissolve. But the modern Court worries over textbooks and bus rides for parochial school children, over voluntary prayer in state-run public schools, over the racial mix in a church-related private college.[7] The modern Court's procrustean use of the No Establishment Clause, in settings it was never intended to fit, has frequently put this Clause and its companion, Free Exercise, in conflict.[8] Lacking any principled way to harmonize them, the Court usually throws up its hands in agony, rubberstamps "separation of church and state is violated" on the law under scrutiny, and appeals to an incantation about "No Establishment means No Establishment, not something else." As this chapter will explain, such "analysis" is a circle, and it is vicious.

Unfortunately, in the twentieth century there has been a marked diminution of interest in the Founders' intent, historical practice, and common sense accommodation in this area. Nowhere is this more obvious than in the secularization of our public schools.

The Secular Humanist Assault on Public Education

For a long time the basic philosophy underlying American education was Christian. The public schools reflected an educational philosophy consonant with parents' Christian conscience. The "three R's" or "content" of education was taught within a shared understanding of nonsectarian Christian principles—a common value scheme. Thus the Northwest Ordinance of 1789 declared:

> Religion, morality, and knowledge being necessary to good government and the happiness of mankind, schools and the means of education shall forever be encouraged.

The "public" schools, which began to spread in the 1840s, were "pan Protestant." They naturally embodied the almost-universal national ethos; they grew out of the society that fostered them as the branches grow from the tree. As an extension of the parents' values, the schools resembled the one depicted on the TV program, "Little House on the Prairie": they had religious and cultural homogeneity, discipline, and "the basics," a teacher drawn from the immediate small community, and support from the local Protestant church. But at this time, before the ecumenical movement and the aggressive hostility of secular humanism, Catholics, Lutherans, Christian Reformed, and some other Protestant groups resented the specific theology of the "nonsectarian" Christian-public schools and felt they had to start their own. These schools too were the natural outgrowth of Christian communities wanting to educate their children in their own faith, without dilution from other brands of Christianity. Interestingly, in an era of still sharp theological disagreement, all Christian groups nonetheless broadly shared the prevailing set of *moral* values, epitomized in the character, for example, of Abraham Lincoln. But these independent schools did not receive any tax support even though parents paid education taxes, and even though by educating thousands of children these schools were, by the 1960s, saving the taxpayers literally millions, if not billions, of dollars.

It seems that this arrangement was always unjust. But those who perpetrated it may be excused, in part, because they did not distinguish between the claims of *churches* and the civic claims of the *parents*. No church has a rightful claim for general tax support for its religious ministry; but every parent does have the same claim for tax support for the *secular* content of his child's education. This is a right which he does not *lose* simply because in conscience he wants that content taught within a Christian value scheme.

There were many reasons why the educational dissenters had to support the pan-Protestant school system with their taxes though they themselves received no benefit of those taxes. First, the dissenters were newcomers often culturally and linguistically not yet "Americanized." Second, the largest group among them, the Catholics, could rely on a pool of nuns and lay brothers to donate their services at mere subsistence wages. Third, the distinction between "value orientation" and "secular content" was not clearly understood by either Protestants or Catholics. Further, during the last century different Christian communions harbored deep historical resentments against one another. Then too, public school taxes were relatively low and independent school tuition was low as well. But perhaps the two main reasons the injustice perdured were, first, that the federal government, with its heightened compulsory exactions and not-too-subtle secular humanism, had not entered the picture and, second, that the public schools as recently as the immediate post-World War II era were both good schools intellectually, and still pan-Protestant and thus solid in terms of basic Christian values. Consequently it was hard to make a persuasive case that these Protestant schools were that harmful to the dissenter's religious conscience, for the public schools did stand up for *basic* Christian values, with their prayer, Bible reading, moralizing McGuffy Readers, teaching of creation, and religious celebrations on feast days. It seemed that the religious dissenters running their own schools were merely adding an unnecessary superstructure deemed by the popular mind to be the peculiar paraphernalia of their sect.

With the close of World War II we entered a thirty-year watershed in education. The era that dawned in 1945 was to contain such shocks to the de facto pan-Protestant establishment that a kind of culture lag still affects the older people today, who remember McGuffy and Bible reading when they were school children. Bluntly, the secular humanists pulled the rug out from under the pan-Protestant control of public schools. To change the metaphor: they assaulted the citadel and it fell. They captured the educational institutions, despite some rear-guard skirmishing by individual teachers around Christmas, in small towns, and in the Deep South.

The three decades since World War II saw a struggle between the retreating majority, who wanted public education to stay basically pan-Protestant, and the attacking secular minority. The minority carried on an assault on two fronts: they would destroy the common-denominator Protestant atmosphere in public schools, and they would largely destroy the financial base for the religiously defined private schools. The secular humanists were aided by the political philosophy of statism, strong in its ideological form in the academies and strong politically in the federal government. The statist viewed schools not as natural extensions of grass roots communities but as a tool of the impersonal state, belonging to a special caste of administrators and experts, benevolently imposed from the top down, as it were, on the ignorant masses, who were incompetent to decide what "good education" really is. This elitist ideology helps explain such follies as the Office of Education campaign to purge textbooks of what it calls "sexism" and its efforts to abolish all-girl basketball teams in Iowa.

The secular humanists also received help from another source. In their fight to prevent Christian schools from receiving a share of their parental supporters' taxes for such unobjectionable neutral subjects as math, modern foreign languages, and physical education, the secular humanists were often abetted by some good Christians who should have been more circumspect about what Prince they were serving. While space does not permit tracing every sortie and sniper in the war, some of the major battles stand out.

One was the 1947 case of *Everson v. Board of Education,* which contains a hyperbole by Justice Black that still taints our thinking in church-state matters:

> The establishment of religion clause of the First Amendment means *at least* this: . . . No tax in *any* amount . . . can be levied to support *any* religious activities or *institutions,* whatever they may be called, or whatever form they may adopt to teach or practice religion. (Emphasis added.)[9]

That American practice for the first century of our national life, as well as, for example, government provision for military chaplains, gave the lie to Black's misreading of history does not trouble those who use his dictum as a weapon. Yet Justice Black himself had neutralized his sweeping prohibition later in the same opinion, where he endorsed the child-benefit theory, which enabled the majority to uphold bus rides for parochial school children. He said that the Free Exercise Clause makes it clear that the state

> cannot hamper its citizens in the free exercise of their own religion. Consequently, it cannot exclude individual Catholics, Lutherans, Mohammedans, Baptists, Jews, Methodists, Non-believers, Presbyterians, or the members of any other faith, *because of their faith, or lack of it,* from receiving the benefits of public welfare legislation. (Italics by the Court.)

But despite upholding the bus rides, the mood of the Court was at least covertly anti-Catholic and possibly even anti-Protestant. This led to the astounding result in *McCollum v. Board of Education* (1948) which struck down the work of an ecumenical group of ministers and a priest, who had developed a voluntary released time religion class program for an hour a week on the public school premises.[10] This program, overwhelmingly satisfactory to the vast majority of the Champaign, Illinois, community, was simply an educational recognition by the schools, as extensions of the parents, that by 1948 society had become sociologically pluralist: there was no longer one "pan-Protestant" set of religious values that satisfied almost everybody. But an atheist plaintiff could not tolerate the fact that the schools could provide even an hour of formal education in the values the taxpaying parents wanted for their children. Now as some jokester put it, this plaintiff, Mrs. McCollum, could have supplied an "atheist chaplain," a latter-day Robert Ingersoll perhaps, to teach her son during his hour of released time. But instead she succeeded in taking away the right of the Protestants, Catholics, and Jews to have *their* ministers teach *their* children. Using a clause in the Constitution designed only to prevent the *federal* government from setting up a *national* church, the Supreme Court struck down a voluntary released time religion class set up by a town in Illinois as an "establishment of religion"!

The outcry was loud. For example, Edwin Corwin, the "dean" of constitutional law scholars, wrote a sharp article entitled, "The Supreme Court as National School Board." But as the magician says as he warms to his act, "You ain't seen nothin' yet."

Secularism in Education: The New Establishment

The decades since *Everson* and *McCollum* have seen the triumph of secular humanism. Indeed, it is no exaggeration to say that secular humanism is functionally the equivalent of a religion and is now the established religion of American public schools.[11] Obviously, this assertion offends people who think or profess to think the public schools are merely neutral. They should look at what secular humanism is.

Secular humanism, in the sense of an exclusive concern for man and human affairs, may be as old as man himself. But its formal explicit promotion is a fairly recent development. There were of course ancient Greeks such as Democritus and Protagoras, and Romans such as Epicurus and Lucretius, who were secular humanists. In the last three centuries, Hobbes, Hume, Holbach, and Feuerbach gave secular humanism its explicit substance, as did certainly Auguste Comte in the last century, with his new "Religion of Humanity," and Karl Marx. The phrase commonly in vogue during this period was "secularism," which the *Oxford Dictionary* defined as "the doctrine that morality should be based solely on regard to the well-being of man in the present life, to the exclusion of all considerations drawn from belief in God or in a future state."[12]

In the twentieth century, secular humanist associations formed in the United States. These embodied a belief that the advance of secular knowledge and science promoted by education should replace traditional religious faiths and morality. Leading American educators such as John Dewey, John Herman Randall, Jr., and Harry Elmer Barnes joined others of like mind in 1933 to issue the *Humanist Manifesto I*, which denied the existence of the supernatural, rejected divine revelation and divine law, and asserted that "religious humanists regard the universe as self-existing and not created."[13] For such outmoded *isms* as Theism and Deism, the *Manifesto* substitutes a new religion, Humanism, whose supreme being is man himself, promising fulfillment exclusively in this world:

> Religious humanism considers the complete realization of human personality to be the end of man's life and seeks its development and fulfilment in the here and now.

The *Manifesto* rejects the idea of an immortal human soul, saying that "traditional dualism of mind and body must be rejected." It also rejects traditional morality, saying:

> The nature of the universe depicted by modern science makes unacceptable any supernatural or cosmic guarantees of human values.

In 1941 American humanists formally set up the American Humanist Association and began to publish the periodical *The Humanist.* In 1963 some clergymen and others with religious interests formed an affiliate, the Fellowship of Religious Humanists. In 1973 the American humanists updated their original creed by publishing *Humanist Manifesto II.* This reiterated the articles of faith of 1933 and emphasized that the obligations of ethics are individual, autonomous, and situational, that is, subjective, depending on the situation. It openly endorsed free love between consenting adults, homosexuality, abortion, and euthanasia.

Their writings show that modern secular humanists are atheists or agnostics who reject Judeo-Christian religious doctrine and the Ten Commandments. They reject the first three Commandments, which require reverence for the Creator, since they deny he exists; the fourth, which says, "Honor thy father and thy mother," by encouraging the young to abandon the moral code of their parents; and the Commandment which forbids murder, for they approve of abortion and euthanasia. Since they view ethics as "autonomous and situational" and allege that "traditional moral codes . . . fail," they can sometimes find reasons to circumvent the Commandments dealing with lying, stealing, coveting, and adultery.

The founders of the American Humanist Movement in 1933 described their beliefs as "a religion." Though some prefer to call it a "philosophy of life," the book *The Philosophy of Humanism* by Corliss Lamont explains how humanism has many characteristics of a religion, including "mysticism," "quest of the ideal," and "supreme commitment." *Humanist Manifesto II* also contrasts humanism with "traditional religions," thus implying it is a form of religion. Members of the Fellowship of Religious Humanists prefer the term "religion" for humanism. Finally, the U.S. Supreme Court, in *Torcaso v. Watkins,* called "secular humanism" a form of "religion," along with other religions which do not profess belief in the existence of God;[14] and, in *U.S. v. Seeger,* has expanded the meaning of "religion" to include one's basic philosophy of life, even if non-theistic.[15]

Among the good points in secular humanism are its stress on the worth of man, human potential, the beauty of the world, the good both of individuals and human society. Its optimism and appreciation of nature are refreshing, as are its commitment to self-improvement, the welfare of society at large, and the betterment of the human condition. It also deserves praise for its opposition to prejudice, superstition, racism, and extreme conservatism. Its determination to use reason and science to improve the world is laudable.

But its outlook and its educational message focus solely on the techniques of daily living in this world. It denies any value to such great teachers and thinkers as Moses and Jesus, and to the accumulated wisdom of man produced by such giants as Plato, Aristotle, Augustine, Descartes, Kant, and Hegel. Its educational perspective is blind to spiritual experience. It offers no hope for the *individual* and precious little motivation for him to sacrifice self-interest for fellow humans less fortunate than he. It denies life has any transcendent goals. It is materialistic, interested in the "psyche" to be plumbed by analysis perhaps, but not in the soul to be uplifted by prayer. It is education without unchanging moral principles, without a model of human perfection, without an answer to our sense of guilt, and with very little—other than cultural momentum—by way of rationale for being truly good. It is an approach to ethics through values clarification without norms to judge which values once clarified are better than others. Secular humanism in education purges all Christian symbolism from the child's experience; it eradicates all moments of prayer from his school day;[16] if it could, it would erase every religious allusion from great literature. Secularistic education approaches human sexuality by demeaning the sacred power of procreation by such bloodless euphemisms as "obtaining the fetus" to describe an abortion, when one really means "killing an unborn child"; speaks of "adolescents being 'sexually active,'" when one really really means "promiscuity"; and of "love," when one really means "lust." It shows studied neutrality to the question whether it is better to be promiscuous or chaste before marriage and faithful or faithless in marriage. Secularistic education gives no reasons to love or care for people who are not attractive; gives no guidance in the hard choices in life; makes no connection with the roots of our Judeo-Christian culture; avoids the inspiring history of the prophets, martyrs, and saints; provides no meaning to sickness, suffering, and death—and passes over in silence, when it does not actually deny, the central concern of the human condition: the fact that we have sinned, and we need, desperately, a Redeemer.

This philosophy, applied to education of the young, is a potent brew. All education inculcates attitudes and moral viewpoints. It does so positively and negatively, directly and indirectly, explicitly and implicitly. All schooling has content which one may test by standardized examinations. All schooling has a value-scheme, the school's answer, by silence or comment, to ultimate questions: Where did I come from? What is the purpose of life? What is good and what is bad? How do I know? Why should I sacrifice for the good and avoid the evil? Is there a God? Is there an afterlife? What is happiness? How do I find happiness in this life and in the next? Though both an independent religious school and a government-run non-religious school will teach the same core content—math is math, whatever the school—they are miles apart on values.

Public school leaders claim to be neutral about the answers to these ultimate questions. Despite the claim, however, public schools admittedly try to inculcate moral values. Thus the annual *Handbook* of the National Education Association regularly contains a resolution titled, "Moral and Ethical Values," which in the 1960s and into the 1970s read:

> The . . . Association believes that an understanding of the American Heritage and the traditional values of the American way of life is a primary goal of teaching and learning in the public schools. The Association recommends that all educators emphasize . . . the application of our moral and ethical values. [It] . . . also urges that schools make every effort to develop in school-age citizens a capacity of moral judgment.

In 1951 the American Association of School Administrators declared:

> The development of moral and spiritual values is basic to all other educational objectives. Education uninspired by moral and spiritual values is directionless. . . . That educational purposes rest on moral and spiritual values has been generally recognized in the public school system.

Such theses may seem unobjectionable at first glance. However, when one inspects what actually goes on in the public schools, he finds only *humanistic* "spiritual" values. Indeed, he may not find even those. Instead, he runs into vapid "values-clarification" exercises: questions and problems—both social and personal—involving morals are proposed for discussion and solution; each student is to make his choice among a variety of options, with the same drifting preoccupation with "getting in touch with one's own feelings" as characterized the psychologists in such TV fiction programs as "The Bob Newhart Show" and "Dallas." The instruction is clear: the key is not whether a course of action is "good" or "bad" in itself, but *how you feel about it* or *how it makes you feel*. Moreover, the classroom instruction in these exercises constantly drifts into sensitive areas, including one's general outlook on life, ideals of honesty and truthfulness, methods of solving social and personal problems, norms concerning the family, ways of dealing with the sex urge, how to relate to members of the opposite sex.

The question of sex identity and sexual morality is one of the main battlegrounds in the schools. Sex education courses routinely describe sexual organs and actions with the same clinical detachment that a plumber would display while explaining how to install a sump pump. The premise of these courses—that knowledge equals virtue, that the more facts the teenagers get the more responsible will be their decisions—is foolish; one might as well explain to a group of potential arsonists how to light matches. To say that sex education will not make children more eager to "try it" denies the lessons of experience. Claims of neutrality about virtue and vice in these courses is a hoax. What the teacher is teaching is this: we do not care if unmarried teenagers commit fornication as long as no pregnancy results; we do not know if it is morally wrong; we have no way to help you decide. Needless to say, this agnosticism is secular humanism, pure—or should I say, impure—and simple.

In a traditional course such as literature, the clash of values is often just as acute. For example, in Shakespeare's play *Julius Caesar*, the tragic hero, Marcus Brutus, the "noblest Roman of them all," joins the conspiracy against Caesar and, despite misgivings, cooperates in stabbing him to death—all for the good purpose, Brutus convinces himself, of saving the Republic from a would-be dictator. "Does the end justify the means?" the students will ask. The secularist teacher will have to answer, "Sometimes—it depends." Again, Brutus ends his life by suicide to prevent capture by Marc Anthony. "Can it ever be moral to commit suicide?" the students ask. A Christian would answer, "No, because you belong, in the final analysis, to God." But how did the "noblest Roman of them all" answer? How would the secular humanist answer? Will the students hear a sympathetic explanation of the Christian answer? It is doubtful. The Supreme Court has held that a public school cannot even post the Ten Commandments in the classroom.

The Supreme Court, in fact, has become the engine driving

the relentless secularization of the schools.[17] To summarize the results, in the last thirty-five years it has become unconstitutional to release children for a couple of hours for voluntary religious study in school, read the Bible, recite a short nonsectarian prayer at the start of the school day, and post the Ten Commandments. Following the Supreme Court's lead, lower courts have done such things as preventing the Gideons from using the public schools for momentary storage when distributing Bibles to voluntary recipients,[18] proscribing Christmas cribs and displays, silencing teachers who want to read, without comment, the nativity narration just prior to Christmas,[19] and pressuring schools to secularize their Christmas pageants. Very few school libraries contain many expressly Christian books—but many, in the larger cities at least, have books containing pornographic material.

Again, though all the world's great religions teach various methods of prayer and many deal in mystical experience, you will not find a single course about prayer in a public school. "Current Ideas" courses are more likely to feature discussions of the pro-abortion and anti-pornography decisions of the courts, dilemmas of doctors and relatives concerning the survival of suffering people lacking hope of recovery, the rights of gay people, and the proper legal status of marijuana. "Values" discussions often focus on such issues as "Constructing a Life Philosophy," "The Sexual Revolution," and "Problems of Death." Teachers conduct imaginative "Future Planning Games" on such topics as "Changing Family Sex Roles and Concepts" and "The Changing Role of Religion," in which the teachers' guides inevitably stress flexibility and relativism. *The assumption in such discussions is that a group or society can eliminate human life on the basis of a utilitarian pragmatic calculus.*

In public schools such values problems are "solved" without reference to religious or transcendent teaching. The peer group and teacher pressure assures a merely secularist approach. For example, in a costly, well-illustrated, skillfully presented course, "Man: A Course of Study" for fifth graders, prepared with federal tax funds and used extensively in public schools, practices among certain Eskimos, such as adultery, wife-swapping, infanticide, cannibalism, and elimination of the useless elderly, traditionally deemed immoral, are presented for open-ended class discussion, with judgments promoting "broad-minded toleration."

Though there be no predetermined or teacher-dictated solutions to such discussions, they still inculcate certain values and erode other values. Immature students learn that various viewpoints have equal status without any set solution. This "neutral" approach is not neutral at all, for it conveys the impression there is no definite, permanent, fundamental moral law. It implicitly rejects divine revelation as a source of moral rules. With all alternatives made equal, the students come to assume that individual human reason can establish or discard moral laws, and that revealed religion and morality are invalid and superfluous. Thus young children, with very limited knowledge, are invited to substitute the value judgments of their peers or of the teacher for those of parents and traditional religion.

Silence teaches too. If a parent were scrupulously to avoid all reference to religion and morality in the upbringing of his children and were to omit any reference to religious teaching in handling basic ethical dilemmas when instructing his children, he would be said to be denying the existence of God and the value of religion. So also with the schools—with this difference: the American public schools protest that they teach everything children need to know for success. Surely the smorgasbord curriculum teaches every facet of life—from brushing teeth, typing, hygiene, sex, writing good sentences, reading French— suggesting that the educators are making sure students do not miss *anything* important. The school becomes surrogate parent; its authority is pervasive. The school teaches that if anything is skipped it is too unimportant to be taken. But religion and the Bible are skipped.

In Supreme Court cases already noted, the Court treated secular humanism as a religion and defined "religion" to embrace those ultimate ethical commitments that hold the place of religion in one's values—that is, one's subjective viewpoint on those ultimate questions. Clearly what the public schools are doing is de facto what the Court described in those cases. At least what the schools do is far closer to what the humanists want taught than it is to what evangelicals, traditional Catholics, and other Christian groups want their children to learn. Moreover, the present state of affairs is the product of thirty to fifty years of aggressive political and litigational labors by groups whose *official, publicly stated philosophy is secular humanism.* It is an axiom in philosophy that the Cause transmits something of its nature to the Effect; the Effect is in some sense a replica of the Cause. Whether one argues from the results in the schools or from the position of the activists who brought about those results, the conclusion is the same: the secular humanist philosophy is the dominant philosophy/religion in our public schools.

This being so, why does the Supreme Court not admit it? There are several reasons. One is that very few cases have presented the argument with adequate starkness. Second, many of the Supreme Court Justices have themselves contributed to the establishment of secular humanism, and it would be too much to expect them to admit what they have done. Third, the pretense of "neutrality" must be maintained. If the Court were to admit that secularism is now established, it would follow that the government is aiding a religion. This is not permitted. What is at stake is nothing less than the funding of all the public schools. An admission that the schools are not neutral, that they have substituted secular humanism for their erstwhile pan-Protestantism, would mandate a ruling that government abandon school financing, that the public schools stop taking compulsory taxes and begin to charge tuition. At least such an admission would mandate that the government pay—probably on a per-pupil basis—as much tax money for children in private schools as in public schools. This would destroy the public school monopoly on finance. Yet many public school supporters live off that monopoly and do sincerely believe that their public schools are the only way to "Americanize" the next generation. They are terrified that the public schools might simply melt away—as the Wicked Witch of the West did in the *Wizard of Oz* when Dorothy threw water on her. Though they teach "survival of the fittest" in their evolution courses, the public schools do not want to have to practice it.

Private School Financing and the State

The court decisions that effectively erased the pan-Protestant atmosphere of the public schools accomplished one goal of the secularists. Another series of court rulings accomplished the second goal—to destroy the financial base for religiously motivated private schools.

Anticipating the burdens if independent schools were to close and send their students into the public schools, many state legislatures have devised different forms of aid for secular education in independent schools. A decade ago Pennsylvania attempted to pay for the services of the teachers in the private schools who offered math, modern foreign languages, and physical education. But the Supreme Court scuttled this attempt in *Lemon v. Kurtzman* (1971).[20] In *Meek v. Pittenger* (1975),[21] the Court struck down even "neutral, non-ideological" aid such as "auxiliary" educational equipment, despite the fact that the quoted phrase was drawn from *Lemon,* where the Court had used it with approval. In *Comm. for Pub. Education v. Nyguist,*[22] the Court objected to subsidies for maintenance and repair of buildings (despite Black's second *Everson* dictum) and reimbursement of parents for a percentage of tuition. In many of these and other cases the Supreme Court shows scarce regard for the factual record or, worse, simply disregards that record and indulges in conjecture about *possible* evils that *could* follow.[23]

Finally, in a complicated way that defies easy summary, the Supreme Court in 1977 modified *Meek* slightly in *Wolman v. Walter.*[24] Here a shifting majority upheld parts of a six-sided $88,000,000 Ohio law giving non-public school children peripheral benefits such as speech therapy; but only Justices Burger and Rehnquist fully perceived the injustice in denying educational finance to student citizens simply because of their religion.

Yet the Court must kick against its own goad. For it has long recognized the prior claim of parental conscience to control both secular content and spiritual value-orientation in their children's education. In *Pierce* (1925), a unanimous Supreme Court stated:

> The fundamental theory of liberty upon which all governments in this Union repose excludes any general power of the State to standardize its children by forcing them to accept instruction from public teachers only. The child is not the mere creature of the State; those who nurture him and direct his destiny have the right, coupled with the high duty, to recognize and prepare him for additional obligations.[25]

In *Wisconsin v. Yoder* (1972), the Court exempted Amish children from compulsory public school attendance, and spoke with approval of the parents' prior right to educate

> to moral standards, religious beliefs, and elements of good citizenship [and pointed out that] the interests of parenthood are combined with a free exercise claim.[26]

Yet by its tax system, the state forces all citizens to pay for the content *and the value scheme* in the state-run schools educating the public but refuses to permit any funds for the content, much less the value scheme, in the independent schools also educating the public. Thus the Christian parent who wants to take seriously the Lord's Last Supper discourse about the vine and the branches, the parent who wants his *own* value orientation rather than that of the secular humanists to influence his children, faces a cruel choice. He has a *right* to both secular subject content (the legislature has given it) *and* his religious values (the Supreme Court has declared it). But if he chooses his tax money for the content, he must give up the demands of his conscience; if he follows his conscience and chooses a private school, he must give up his tax money. To make a citizen give up one right in order to obtain another right that others have without any such sacrifice is clearly unjust.

Critics of public aid to private schools say, "I do not want to aid *your* religion." My response is that every citizen has the duty to help a child learn the *secular* subjects in *whatever context is congenial to his parents' conscience*. Any incidental benefit to religion of such aid is balanced by comparable incidental benefit to non-religion in schools that are secularist.

A second objection, one which Christians sometimes urge, is that "We don't want government aid anyway. We are rugged individualists. We'll do without." My response is that a vow of poverty is meritorious only if it is voluntary. But we are talking justice, not charity. If you want to do charity to your fellow taxpayers by not claiming tax money which is yours by *right*, that is your privilege. I admire your austerity. But it is unjust not to give the religious parent *the choice* whether he wants his own tax money to support his children's education. Moreover, the practical consequence of one's vow of personal poverty in this case is the impoverishment of others; there are too many people with large families, on low income, or who face costly "accreditation standards" who cannot afford private schools. If we Christians refuse to claim our civic rights from an increasingly hostile Leviathan state, we reduce religiously oriented education to the luxury of the rich. We should devise a system of justice wherein each parent can use his own tax money for his own child's education; then, if someone does not want his share, he can give it to his church's missionary work or some other good cause.

Many proposals have been advanced to restore a measure of fairness to educational finance and give practical encouragement to religious free exercise. Let us outline some of them.[27]

First, we could stop all public financing of schools and allow the free market to work. This was the general approach in

America from 1776 till roughly 1840. Considering the vitality of private schools even though their competition is subsidized by tax money, there is no doubt that private enterprise in education would work. Both proprietary and non-profit schools would spring up to augment those already existing; with their property taxes reduced fifty to seventy percent because no longer claimed by public schools, parents would have adequate funds to pay for these private schools. Parents would have far more control and choice, lower costs, and surely a higher level of literacy. Realistically, however, this radical reversal of practice will not happen.

Second, we could stop *increasing* taxes to pay for increasing public school costs and begin to charge modest tuition for them. This policy would begin to narrow the cost differential between government-run public schools and privately run public schools. The public schools would begin to compete on a relatively fair basis. To the extent that public schools charge tuition, to that degree Christian taxpayers would not have to subsidize secular humanist teaching. There is nothing sacrosanct about "free" public schools. Indeed, the layers of bureaucratic consultants, advisors, and administrators piled on top of classroom teaching exist in part because there is little financial discipline forcing a reduction in waste.

Third, we could permit taxpayers to designate which schools would receive their education taxes. Such a system would be the most equitable. Everyone would still have to pay for the content of education, but each citizen could choose the context, the value-orientation, which most accorded with his own conscience. A parent of school-age children would have to pay his education taxes to whichever accredited school he prefers. Lutherans, Evangelicals, Catholics, and others would presumably support Lutheran, Evangelical, Catholic, and other schools. The parents, not any church, would be in control: if the religious-minded taxpayer did not find the religious makeup of the school to his liking, he could take his money and his child elsewhere, or he could form his own school. Such a system would encourage an explosion of creativity, as groups of educated persons set up their own schools without the present hindrance of financial suffocation. Presumably, if they were not so eager to establish their own philosophy as the official ideology of the state, secular humanists like Mrs. McCollum and Robert Ingersoll would be able to find numerous schools reflective of their values, and they too would be happy. Comparable systems obtain in parts of Canada and Holland. It would torture logic, too, to find an "establishment of religion" in an arrangement that treated equally the views of Martin Luther, Thomas Aquinas, Billy Graham, and Robert Ingersoll.

Fourth, instead of the local government or state sending the tax money to the school, we could, on the state level, give the taxpayer a tax credit against real estate taxes for the amount of money he chooses to donate to any school of his choice. Here we cut the nexus between state and school by interposing the parent-taxpayer as the direct source of the funds.

Fifth, on the state or federal level we could enact a G.I.-Bill-type "voucher system" whereby government pays a direct grant to each parent with school children. To avoid the charge of preference for religiously oriented schools, this approach should be coupled with initiation of fees or modest tuition by the public schools so that all parents would have education costs the voucher would reduce. The original G.I. Bill enabled veterans going to college to take their government-provided grant to Notre Dame or Southern Methodist or any accredited school of their choice. When government subsidizes the consumers of the "educational groceries" rather than the suppliers, it is no one's business what "grocery store" the consumer-students patronize, as long as they are being intellectually nourished.

Sixth, Congress could pass tax credits against federal income taxes. The Congress is inclined to such a solution, but its political viability is crippled somewhat by the intransigence of the teachers' unions, who want to monopolize everybody's education tax money, and by militant secular humanists, whose ideological triumph over the last thirty years would be reversed.

A tax credit is a subtraction from income tax owed; unlike a reduction, which reduces the "taxable income," a credit reduces the tax itself. If a parent were to pay $1,200 tuition to a private school, and he had a credit up to $500, his income tax is reduced by $500 because he spent the money on a governmentally approved purpose—education. If he had a tax credit of fifty percent of tuition, he would save $600 in taxes. If there were a tax credit of, say, fifty percent of all gifts to any school, and he gave $300 to the local Evangelical Christian School, he would be able to subtract $150 from his federal income tax. So also would a person who gave, perhaps through the P.T.A., $300 to his local public school.

The fact that the proposed credits are usually against tuition tends to becloud the argument. In reality this is quite fair, since tuition is a *second* payment for education, the first being most of local property taxes and part of the citizen's state and federal income taxes; and the credit only reduces, in small part, that second payment. But because students do not pay tuition in public schools, opponents smokescreen the equity argument by calling credits special aids for a "minority" segment of people. They conveniently overlook the special aid the majority have already received by "free" tax-subsidized government-school education. Still, the tax credit's basic fairness is a compelling point for many. One would think that a tax credit for free-will *donations* up to, say, $500 per year per school for private *and public* schools would be no more subject to honest constitutional attack than is tax deductibility of donations to churches. At this writing, the Supreme Court has not yet spoken on the issue, although it has set a pertinent case for argument in the 1982-83 Term of Court. Because the Court has painted itself into a rhetorical corner by its overly expansive dicta about the meaning of the Establishment Clause, I will not predict the outcome. Though "equal protection" is unfortunately not a theme usually struck in church-state cases, a congressional or state effort to give *all* independent schools a few crumbs from its abundant table of school subsidies should be seen as simple justice. But when ideology rules, dogma sometimes impedes common sense.

Christians who support private education should not under-estimate the hostility private schools engender among the secular elite. The very existence of Christian schools annoys secular humanists. These schools stand for values that come from outside society and government—for parental control, not bureaucratic management. The recent growth of Christian schools witnesses to the fact that many citizens no longer believe the exaggerated claims of the public schools. The consumers of a product offered free by the state refuse to accept it; they go to private suppliers and pay a high price. Many of the rule-makers of society resent this.

The depth of this resentment was on display in the fall of 1978 when the Internal Revenue Service decided to take hold of the Christian schools. It may be that the tax collectors' purposes were benign, but the result, had they succeeded, would have been the Final Solution to the Christian Problem in education.

On August 22, 1978, the I.R.S. published in the *Federal Register* a "proposed Revenue Procedure on Private Tax-Exempt Schools."[28] This "procedure" was actually a substantive rule; it proposed automatic loss of tax exemption for all private schools if found "discriminatory" by a court *or agency,* or if they lacked a "minority" student enrollment of twenty percent of the "minority school population" of the *public* school district in which the private school was located. Further, the proposal set up a *presumption* that the private school is discriminatory if it fails to have, among other things, "an increasing percentage of minority student enrollment" and "employment of minority teachers." The only way the school could rebut this presumption would be to carry "the burden of clearly and convincingly" demonstrating that it did not discriminate on racial grounds. It would be only "rare and unusual" to find a school not enrolling some minority students to be non-discriminatory.

The I.R.S. had been claiming that there are about 100 private schools which discriminate racially in the United States. This figure is probably overblown, but even if true, it scarcely justifies bureaucratic regulations affecting over 3,500 Roman

Catholic, Lutheran, Christian Reformed, Evangelical, and other Bible-based schools. Something is amiss when 3,500 have to prove their innocence because 100 might be guilty. To generalize a negative trait and claim it taints an entire group because a few members of that group have the trait is the essence of bigotry and prejudice; yet the I.R.S. based its proposed rule-change on just such a generalization—ironically, in the name of attacking bigotry and prejudice!

The I.R.S. "twenty percent rule" meant that a private religious school in a city whose public schools were seventy percent black would have to have fourteen percent of its own student body drawn from that minority because $.20 \times .70 = .14$. Such a racial mix may well be desirable, but the rule has no support in common sense. It is absurd to use a whole public school district as the basis for the fraction in judging whether a private school therein has enough "Blacks, Hispanics, Asians or Pacific Islanders, and American Indians or Alaskan Natives," as the Revenue Procedure put it. One might as well ask whether United Air Lines, headquartered in Cook County, Illinois, carries among its passengers a certain percentage of minorities based on twenty percent of the minority citizens of Chicago.

The reason, as certainly the I.R.S. knew or could have discovered, is the self-selection among students of independent schools. These schools charge tuition; most minority people are disadvantaged and cannot afford tuition. Such students get free access to public schools, usually in better facilities with higher-paid teachers than private school students. Moreover, about ninety percent of the private schools put religion as central to their teaching. Because of this they attract a certain constituency—and repel others. Yet under the I.R.S. reliance on statistics to determine discriminatory intent, the tax authorities could remove tax exemption from a Mormon school in Hawaii because it lacked a percent of "Pacific Islanders," most of whom are not Mormon; from a Catholic school in the South Side of Chicago because lacking a percent of blacks, most of whom are not Catholic; and from an Evangelical school in a Hispanic community where most are Catholics.

In fairness, the I.R.S. should have admitted that private schools cannot be expected to reflect any specific quota of minority enrollment, any more than any enterprise charging a price for its service in a market could be expected to sell that service to an exact percentage of its potential clientele, especially when a competitor—here the public schools—provides the same service free. Why did the I.R.S. pick twenty percent rather than fifteen percent or twenty-five percent? Why did it specify the entire school district rather than the public school population within the boundaries of the private school's natural reach, such as a parish school's boundaries? In one section (#.05 appearing on p. 37297) it was stated:

> If there is *any* evidence that a school in fact has a racially discriminatory policy or practice, the Service [may remove the exemption] without regard to whether the school has complied with the guidelines set forth in this revenue procedure. [Emphasis added.]

Thus if one student complained, say, that he was passed over for a scholarship or perhaps was denied a role in the school play because of his race—this would be "any" evidence—the school would lose its exemption whatever its compliance with the quotas. A simple allegation, a newspaper article, or a letter from a dismissed teacher would suffice.

Yet the burden on the defense was far heavier. "Mere denial of a discriminatory purpose is insufficient" for defense, said the Revenue Procedure text. Rather, the school had to demonstrate either (1) actual enrollment of minority students (the twenty percent rule) or (2) "operation in good faith on a racially nondiscriminatory basis as evidenced by at least four out of five factors." These factors included the racial mix among the teachers and the treatment of racial matters in the curriculum. Thus an agency of government would decide whether the "right" teacher or textual treatment were present. Such a policy is an obvious violation of academic freedom and of the parents' constitutional right to free exercise of religion.

It is a sad commentary on the professionalism of our journalists that the public now has the impression that the prime reason for the burgeoning Christian school movement is a racist desire to avoid integrated public schools. The truth is that Christians overwhelmingly reject racial discrimination. Virtually all religious private schools have longstanding—and financially costly—policies of welcoming minorities. The truth is that the student exodus from the public schools of our country is due to their lack of discipline, silence about values, permissive sex education, uncontrolled drug culture, undemanding assignments, dropping SAT scores, smorgasbord electives, divorcement from tradition, watered down patriotism, and absence of commitment to Jesus Christ. Not all of the public schools are at fault to the same degree, of course; but enough of them are at fault that many repel rather than attract.

What Christians Must Do

Christians must approach the decisions and actions involved in educating their children with a clear understanding of the Lord's teaching in this matter. During the Last Supper, the Lord gave a soliloquy which is possibly the most extraordinary statement in religious literature. It also contains a summary of Christian educational philosophy.

I am the way, and the truth, and the life; no one comes to the Father but by me. If you had known me, you would have known my Father also. (Jn 14:6-7)

"The way" is a road, a path, a direction with a purpose, leading "from here" on along "to there." The correct path excludes all others; the child who takes it does not go off the road or into a dead end. Christ is the correct path. He is the only safe path. The Christian life is a journey. We are pilgrims. Correct education, education in Christ, guides us to our goal.

"The truth" is identity of the mind with reality, the grasp of things as they are, the fulfillment of the mind's purpose. True Christian education helps us find and dwell in the truth. Without Christ as the heart of education, the mind learns only part of reality, the surface without depth, isolated facts without unifying meaning.

"The life" is the only "lifestyle," as today's jargon has it, that is valid, complete, whole, and fully human because it is open to the spiritual. It is the only life that grows without being twisted, warped, or perverted; the life with power within, in the heart, through the Spirit; the opposite of spiritual death through sin, with its ugliness, loss, and dissolution.

> If you love me, you will keep my commandments. . . . He who has my commandments and keeps them, he it is who loves me. . . . If a man loves me, he will keep my word, and my Father will love him, and we will come to him and make our home with him. (Jn 14:15, 21, 23)

So the Lord as teacher states that knowing and keeping his commandments are vitally important, literal matters of life and death. These are not just "guidelines," as the World would have them; nor "preferences," nor "alternative lifestyles"; they are not "values to be clarified," nor feelings "depending on the situation." They are *commandments*. If the child would have life, he must know and keep the Lord's commandments.

Then we come to the marvelous discussion of grace, with its powerful metaphor of the vine and the branches, a statement of the Christian's purpose and witness:

> I am the vine, you are the branches. He who abides in me, and I in him, he bears much fruit, for without me you can do nothing. . . . By this my Father is glorified, that you bear much fruit, and so prove to be my disciples. (Jn 15:5, 8)

Thus *any* child who has Jesus in him, who loves Jesus, who keeps his commandments, will accomplish much in this life; however painful or poor, however sad or abandoned, however small or overlooked his life may seem, he will glorify the Father and bear much fruit. Here is the answer to the frustrations of loss and setback, to the pain of sickness, poverty, and death. Here is the answer to the world's assertion that only glamor and wealth give worth, and only the "beautiful people" like those we see on our TV screens have any meaning in their lives. Here is the ultimate basis for mental health. Thus true education will have Christ at its heart, and it will give meaning to the child's life. But if his education lacks Christ, he will be able to "do nothing," for he will not bear any fruit:

> If a man does not abide in me, he is cast forth as a branch and withers; and the branches are gathered, thrown into the fire and burned. (Jn 15:6)

Christian education teaches the child that love is central, not just the wishy-washy love of feelings, not just romantic love so glorified by the media and so temporary in practice—but sacrificing love, love of deeds and not just words, love that aspires to go as far as the Lord himself goes, namely, to "lay down one's life for his friends." Thus in Christ's eyes, love has nothing to do with pleasure for oneself, reward in this life; it cannot be random or unstructured, an expression of subjective "liberation" which casts off all restraint, for it must be done as a "friend" of Christ. The touchstone of one's friendship for Christ is whether he does the things Christ has commanded.

The other quality of Christian education, the Lord continues, is a healthy disregard for peer group pressure, for social adjustment, for the standards of the world and all its pragmatism and vacuous self-glorification. Rather, education requires a gutsy courage in the face of the world's scorn and hatred, courage to resist the world and to insist that Christian moral principles are true. The Lord himself foretold that

Christian education must prepare the child for persecution, overt or hidden, direct or subtle:

> If the world hates you, know that it has hated me before it hated you. If you were of the world, the world would love what is its own; but because you are not of the world, but I chose you out of the world, therefore the world hates you.
>
> (Jn 15:18-19)

In sum, what Christ has told us is that education must be concerned with values, principled love, unchanging truth, firm morality, discovery of the will of God, and pursuit of our eternal destiny. Note that Christ has not discussed educational content in terms of secular interests in a given society—whether astronomy or zoology, whether the "three R's" or cooking and painting, whether history and literature or math and chemistry. All of these subjects can be taught within a Christian value scheme. I would argue that they can be taught fully and comprehensively only within such a Christian framework.

In his discourse at the Last Supper, the Lord asks the Father to preserve his apostles present—all except Judas, who had left to go out into the night—to preserve his "little children" from the world, which they were to be "in" but not "of." I believe the Lord saw all history to come in one divine vision that night. He saw the militant secular humanism of our age and the education it would foster.

It should be clear by now that this militant secular humanism has conquered the public schools and now threatens even Christian schools. In recent years the calls have been close. The 1978 I.R.S. Revenue Procedure was never adopted because Congress denied the agency the funds to enforce it. But it is likely that a similar attempt to attack private schools will occur again.[29] The I.R.S. move was not "a big mistake," but rather part of an ominous trend. It took place in a wider context of widespread government harassment of Christian organizations and educational institutions. For example, during the later 1970s, roughly the same period as I.R.S. was formulating its regulations, the National Labor Relations Board was reversing a forty-year policy and attempting to assert jurisdiction over teachers' unions in Catholic schools. It wanted to insert itself, a secular entity, as the arbiter in private disputes which could entail questions about the faith or morals of unionized teachers in those schools. This effort was stopped only by a ruling from the Supreme Court. Again, during the 1970s accreditation authorities in Kentucky, Ohio, Vermont, and North Carolina started to interpret their dictionary-long "standards" so as to force private Evangelical Christian schools to close and, in some cases, to justify jailing the parents for "contributing to the delinquency of minors"![30] These attacks on independent schools took place at the same time as the public school curriculum was adopting sex education and the vapid "values clarification" approach to character training.

There is a pattern in all this. The state wants our children. It cannot brook dissent. In its view, government is the primary educator; parents are subordinate, even superfluous and dispensable. The state in modern times wants to resemble the church in medieval times; it would become the basic institutional educator. The modern state is equipped for the job; it has its own pedagogy, values, authority, purposes, and doctrine. It does not recognize the fact that God has given the children to their parents and charged parents with the duty to raise the children in his ways. The state neither desires nor allows God's reality and his claims to limit its collective freedom to make policy in accord with some hedonistic calculus of ostensible benefit for the multitudes. Also, it would be naive not to recognize that state domination of education works to the status and material advantage of its own elite ruling groups. In education, these groups include professional educators, curriculum-revisors, consultants, resource persons, accreditation authorities, full-time administrators, tenured teachers, union leaders, a large segment of academia, and the political allies of all these groups. Whatever the probity of their own lives, and one should acknowledge that many of these people are truly public-spirited and honorable, their institutional purpose, for probably the majority of them, is to obtain and hold onto privilege: *they* will decide how the next generation thinks and, to a large extent, what it thinks about. They will retain their already considerable power. By and large, however, these people are not born-again Evangelicals or traditional Catholics.

When I urge these conclusions in lectures before Christian groups, someone usually rises to declare that the case is overstated, that the public schools are not much different today than when he or she attended them thirty years ago, that Christians should simply "get active" in local school politics and that would "change things." Behind this view lies, I think, considerable psychological frustration. These Christians know something has gone badly wrong with the public schools. They feel the distress of a man whose well-bred child has gone wrong, the self-reproach of a woman who has been taken in by a fast-talking con man, the sadness of the spouse betrayed. For we Americans have been good to our public schools; we have lavished money on them in grand proportions, as much as eighty percent of local property taxes and more recently epic sums from state and federal taxes. By and large over the first half of this century the public schools have reciprocated this generosity. They graduated well-trained students whose spiritual and moral character reflected the grassroots goodness of the parents and school teachers who guided them along paths of common values and righteousness. To be told now that the schools no longer educate the way we indulgent taxpayers want them to is a bitter pill to swallow. Hearing this news rends our hearts the way the heart of the Prodigal Son's father must have grieved when he first learned how his son had spent the inheritance. Neither do we want to hear the corollary of this news—that the benevolent government, to which we give so much in taxes and from which we expect so much in services, is now hostile to our values. We close our ears because we fear the message might be true.[31] That truth, on the one hand, is implicit criticism of the way Christians have carried out their civic responsibilities during the watershed years when we lost our grip on our schools and our government. The truth, on the other hand, is a trumpet call to Do Something. And Doing Something will mean sacrifice—of time, money, and favor in the community.

It should be apparent that those of us who believe the Lord is the way, the truth, and the life must make common cause in the face of this secularist attack.[32] If we believe together that he is the vine and that we and our children are the branches, we must meet the attack together. If as Christians we take seriously Christ's teaching on the importance of unchanging values, principled love, perennial truth, firm morality, primacy of the will of God, and prayerful pursuit of our eternal destiny, then we must act. We should set aside any lingering ill feelings from the past and work together in every forum to argue the cause of justice for all parents.

The struggle for the schools goes on in two theaters: law and education. In law, Christian lawyers must get involved. The litigators must litigate, the scholars write, the speakers speak out. The very existence and independence of private religious schools are ultimately questions of the way the law will treat them. If tough advocates for these schools do not enter the contest before county councils, school boards, local courts, commissions, legislatures, Congress, and the Supreme Court, then the religious schools' adversaries will push the law into policies even more hostile than those at present. As attorney John W. Whitehead has written:

> Christian lawyers need to organize in local attorney groups not only to fellowship but to strategize on how they can influence their community. Imagine a strong Christian lawyers' group threatening legal action against abortion clinics or upholding the right of a Christian teacher to talk about Christ in the public school classroom.[33]

If, for example, Christian lawyers would bring as many lawsuits demanding "equal time" for biblical morality in the sex education classes as did the secular humanists litigate to remove prayer and even the Ten Commandments from the schools, school boards would be more careful—even if the Christians lost in court—in promoting promiscuity through these courses. But the key, as Whitehead points out, is to take the initiative, not just react. Meantime, in the public schools, hedonism takes the place of self-discipline in part because, again, the Christian alternative lacks numerous legal advocates for its position.

In education, we should take practical steps to provide alternative education for our children when we can. The best strategy, it seems to me, is to form nonprofit educational corporations with boards of directors composed of those who agree on basic Christian theology and pedagogy, scout around for suitable temporary quarters, and—always in prayer—start one's own school. Since children in early grades are less likely than junior high and high school students to be harmed by non-Christian education, a school on tight finances should probably start with the seventh and eighth grades. If a group of Christians set up a junior high school for fifty or sixty students the first year and a like number in the second year, this group of roughly one hundred to one hundred twenty families could spearhead the formation of a Christian high school. The school should embody some important principles: admit members of all races, admit members of all creeds, insist on rigorous intellectual training, offer scripture studies taught by believers for all students, encourage members of denominations different from the founding group to instruct their children in their distinctive traditions. Also, because of the likely eventual need to rely on the Free Exercise Clause as a shield against government attack, the school's founders should make sure the articles and by-laws are clear about the religious witness which motivates setting up this school.

What I propose is a modern adaptation of the ecumenical teaching approach widely used in the public schools until the *McCollum* case (1948). There the pan-Protestant public schools in Champaign, Illinois, permitted teachers from the major faiths among the townsfolk to enter the public schools periodically to offer doctrinal instruction to children whose parents had requested it. This could be done again today in private schools in areas where no one denomination has enough members that they can bear the financial burden of the school alone. Needless to say, a large and strong Christian congregation may well decide to "go it alone" with its own school. But I am convinced that the Lord wants Christians of all faiths to bury the hatchet over historical and juridical disagreements, not because these are unimportant, but because fighting past fights distracts from dealing with present problems. If these disputes prevent action, our children are the casualties.

It seems to me that if Christians love the Lord more than they disagree with each other, there should be room for cooperation, in faith and in charity, on the common enterprise of providing a godly education to our children. We should be more concerned than we have been that our fellow Christians have the opportunity to educate their children according to their Christian conscience. Our efforts to serve the Lord and our children should be characterized more by charity and cooperativeness than by excluding certain children or by insisting that they learn a certain type of Christian doctrine despite their parents' wishes. Further, the common Christian commitment to biblical morality, shared by Evangelicals and most Roman Catholics, should make it possible for Evangelical-Catholic cooperation in some circumstances. It would be better for these two groups to work together and set up a school, than to shun each other and have the children of both traditions remain in the public schools.

The Lord wants his "little ones" to come to know, love, and serve him with their whole hearts and minds and wills and all their strength. We Christians should explore any educational method, including cooperation with Christians whose creedal formula we may not fully accept, to achieve what he wants. For we Christian parents want, when it comes our turn to leave this world, to be able to join Jesus' Last Supper prayer for our own "little children":

I am praying . . . for those whom thou hast given me, for they are thine. . . . Holy Father, keep them in thy name, which thou hast given me. . . . While I was with them, I kept them in thy name, which thou has given me; I have guarded them, *and none of them is lost.* (Jn 17:9-12, italics added.)

SIX

Christianity and the Sexual Revolution

Blessed are the pure in heart, for they shall see God.
—Matthew 5:8

The men said to Lot, "Have you any one else here? . . . bring them out . . . , for we are about to destroy this place, because the outcry against its people has become great before the Lord, and the Lord has sent us to destroy it. —Genesis 19:12-13

ONE OF THE IRONIES of our time is the facile way evil is presented as if it were good. Another is the use of law, which should be an embodiment of reasoned ethics and the best of society's civilizing attempts, to undermine and eradicate perennial values. A third irony is the widespread Christian silence about the first two. These observations will take on substance by examining the "sexual revolution."

The "sexual revolution" encompasses many attitudes and practices. They are familiar to most of us. They include attitudes and practices which divorce sexual activity from biblical principles, which separate sex-as-entertainment from sex-as-procreation, which mock chastity in the unmarried and fidelity in the married, which promote promiscuity among teenagers, which see children as obstacles to "individual fulfillment," which encourage "living together" in place of formal marriage, which deem the family an outmoded system, and which frequently welcome and promote experimental and deviant actions that an older generation considers simply perverse.

Obviously not every person who endorses some of these attitudes and practices will embrace them all. But the common threads holding them together as a cluster of beliefs and actions are two assumptions. First is the assumption that sex is a "private matter" without any public norms or God-given rules; second is the attitude that the primary use of sex is to give momentary pleasure to the individual rather than forge a special bond expressed in a lifetime marriage between one man and one woman who desire, within their resources, to permit God to bless them with children. In fact, the ultimate common denominator among the proponents of the sexual revolution is disinterest in or denial of the Christian view of sexual morality. The sexual revolution, at root, involves practical rejection of the binding sexual norms taught by Jesus Christ.

We should acknowledge that quite a few of our fellow citizens who sympathize with and even embody the sexual revolution themselves are otherwise straight-laced individuals. Many who hold that sexual activity is "a person's own business and nobody else's" are also well-mannered, intelligent, hardworking, and honorable. That they have carved out a normless realm of conduct for themselves where they can do pretty much what they want does not seem to interfere with success in business or to detract from their likability as professional associates or apartment-house neighbors. We should be careful not to misjudge the revolutionaries' subjective mind even while we must, of necessity, judge the revolution as an objective movement and trend.

But while being restrained in faulting individuals, we cannot overlook this extraordinary phenomenon: conduct once universally deemed "wrong" is now so commonplace among such respectable people and is taking place with such little sanction (save for the recently publicized herpes plague) that "right" and "wrong" are blending into a neither-right-neither-wrong agnosticism about morality. Under a different name such attitudes amount to no more than neo-paganism.

As Christians, we should keep our equilibrium about this neo-paganism. There is no great surprise here. Paganism is a spiritual-moral deformity in human cultures not unlike widespread sickness, which is a physical defect afflicting humanity. There are ebbs and flows in human history, times when people are more sick or more well, epochs when plagues and epidemics spread like wild fire, other periods when hygiene, nutrition, and medicine combine to spread physical well-being rather generally throughout the population. In spiritual-moral matters, there have been other periods of debasement and decline, and periods of self-control and high public virtue.

Still, it may be that the current deterioration in morals is qualitatively different from past declines. The pervasive television medium makes it possible to undermine an entire culture, and the use of law as an engine of moral change makes it possible to compress otherwise gradual and partial changes into total and rapid overthrow. The law can support a measure of Christian asceticism, but it also can support the rejection of such restraints and their replacement by aggressive, even predatory hedonism. If the laws compel or even simply condone immorality, the sexual revolution will accelerate, and Christian families will find it enormously difficult, if not impossible, to teach their younger members Christian self-control.

The Reasons for Sexual Control

Most Christians realize hedonism is wrong, but they sometimes feel pangs of regret. Christians cannot get in on all fun, while others freely sample the wares of the sexual revolution, rationalizing that "after all, times change. We can't be old-fashioned Puritans."

This excuse begs the question of what is fashion, old or new, and whether we must adopt all the new-fashioned ways. No doubt our straight-laced ancestors, whether Protestant or Catholic, went to extremes in their zeal to pretend sex was nothing much; but today the purveyors of pop culture go to extremes in their zeal to pretend sex is everything. At least our ancestors had some grasp of proportion and of the dynamics of human nature. Guided by revelation and church teaching, our forebears understood fallen human nature: radically flawed through sin, our nature is *disordered*; this disorder takes the form of unruly passions seeking their own pleasure out of control of the overall direction of mind and spirit. Though the body/soul dichotomy is philosophically imprecise—we are not "ghosts in a machine"—the expression accurately suggests something of an important truth. Incarnate spirits do have "two parts," as it were, and the "lower" must be subjected to the "higher" and both to the Word of the Lord. Moreover, our Christian ancestors realized that man has a purpose, a goal, which our passions can interfere with. Thus they understood that every disorderly tendency, like hijackers fighting to capture an airliner, must come under the control of the pilot and crew, who take the plane to its destination and resist efforts to divert it from its goal.

Christians should practice sexual self-control not because they dislike "fun" or are "hung up" with guilt or because the body is somehow "dirty." The reason lies in God's plan:

> God's plan is to make you holy, and that entails first of all a clean cut with sexual immorality. Everyone of you should learn to control his body, keeping it pure and treating it with respect, and never regarding it as an instrument for self-gratification, as do pagans with no knowledge of God.
> (1 Thes 4:3-5)

The purpose of life is to become holy, which means to put on the mind of Christ Jesus, to replace the "old man" of selfishness with the "new man" of Jesus living in us. Sexual disorder absorbs the whole man; it dissipates his energies in short-term pursuit of pleasure. The sensualist is absorbed in himself; he is blind to the Creator and to the things of the spirit. Like a man sinking into quicksand, he soon is sucked down into the muck instead of moving along the path to his goal.

You must no longer live as the Gentiles do, in the futility of their minds; they are darkened in their understanding, alienated from the life of God because of the ignorance that is in them, due to their hardness of heart; they have become callous and have given themselves up to licentiousness, greedy to practice every kind of uncleanness. (Eph 4:17-19)

Failure to restrain the sex drive has some horrible spiritual consequences: first, blindness; then, death. The judgment on Sodom is symbolic:

Before the guests [two angels, visiting Lot] went to bed, the men of Sodom surrounded the house. All the men of the city, both young and old, were there. . . . [They] wanted to have sex with them. . . . They pushed Lot back and moved up to break down the door. But the two men inside reached out, pulled Lot back into the house and shut the door. Then they struck all the men outside with blindness. . . . [The next day] the Lord rained burning sulfur on the cities of Sodom and Gomorrah and destroyed them and the whole valley, along with all the people there. (Gn 19:4, 9-11, 24)

God's anger is due less to the fact that people break his rules than to the fact that they make it impossible to achieve the purpose for which he created them—a purpose in which God has invested an infinite amount of love and suffering to help us achieve. He wants to wake us up to the supernatural. Yet we make that impossible by refusing to control our passions:

For those who live according to the flesh set their minds on the things of the flesh, but those who live according to the Spirit set their minds on the things of the Spirit. To set the mind on the flesh is death, but to set the mind on the Spirit is life and peace. For the mind that is set on the flesh is hostile to God; it does not submit to God's law, indeed it cannot; and those who are in the flesh cannot please God.
(Rom 8:5-8)

The carnal attitude results in self-enslavement. Under the guise of "sexual liberation" the carnal man or woman loses control of self. This is the sanction when we violate our nature, but it is hard to explain without resorting to figures of speech, such as a forest fire out of control or the tamed jungle animal that reverts to the wild. When carnal men refuse to tame their passions and quench the lust that burns within, God abandons them:

> Therefore God gave them up in the lusts of their hearts to impurity, to the dishonoring of their bodies among themselves. (Rom 1:24)

When God abandons people, they lose their freedom, for they need his help in keeping spiritual equilibrium:

> "All things are lawful for me," but I will not be enslaved by anything.... The body is not meant for immorality.... Shun immorality. (1 Cor 6:12, 13, 18).... But you cannot say that our physical body was made for sexual promiscuity. . . . Avoid sexual looseness like the plague. (1 Cor 6:13, 18)

The world's view of sexual taboos notwithstanding, traditional moral standards—chastity before marriage, fidelity in marriage—actually liberate. When a person disciplines himself, he can focus his energies on his only goal—salvation—and thus be freer than the profligate person.

The dissolute lifestyle deadens moral sensibility. Repeated violations of the moral order soon stifle the conscience and choke off one's aspiration to higher spiritual values or purposes. The libertine becomes spiritually flabby, soft, out of shape; he has no time for prayer and he avoids self-discipline. He fails to take the necessary purgative steps that are conditions of the spiritual life. No one reaches God on his own, but humans must remove the obstacles to the action of the Spirit. These steps require asceticism; they are essential preparations for the action of God. Prayer, fasting, almsgiving, corporal works of mercy, obedience to the commandments and to one's calling in life are all necessary "training." But the person who pursues pleasure for its own sake obviously has no time for prayer or fasting. Two of the main components of a life of prayer—a lively faith and firm control of the imagination—both become impossible for the self-debauched. He denies whatever is left of his faith with every new sexual sin and so fills his experience with real or vicarious sexual activities that his imagination turns into a storehouse of a thousand trashy images of debauchery come back to distract him whenever he feebly gropes toward the supernatural.

The Anti-Child Mentality

The sexual revolution arrived when people began to routinely think of sex as primarily a means of entertainment without a further purpose, such as the forming of permanent families through the responsible nurturing of children. They separated sexual activity from procreation and began to play with sex as though it had no natural rules or commands from God.

For a child, play does not *do* anything. Play is play. It is basically immanent action designed to accomplish no more than entertain and perhaps educate the player. When an adult male considers himself a "playboy" and his companions "playmates," he must revise ethics and biology so that the "play" does not bring forth an unwanted result, such as responsibility for a helpless baby. Such responsibility requires a permanent commitment on the part of playboy and playmate to stop "playing" long enough to get down to the real business of sacrificing for the sake of others.

I do not know whether the coming of the playboy brought about widespread use of contraceptives by unmarried people or whether this use caused the coming of numerous playboys. Probably each helped produce the other, just as in economics supply and demand interact causally. Whatever the various causes, for the first time in history there are now simple techniques for totally and permanently severing private sex acts from communal consequences. Today we have the total separation of individual sexual conduct from a public ethic of sexual relations. The shared universe of communal values is shattered. This development bodes ill for secular society and threatens Christians with an unbridgeable dilemma: either be exiled and ostracized from the new permissive norms of society, or adopt them and lose your soul.

Two years ago a law student wrote a research paper for me on the topic of abortion. She was a "liberated woman" who had lived with her boyfriend until their breakup a year earlier. She came to the assignment with all the enthusiasms of the trendy intellectuals of our time. But as the task progressed I admired her honesty, because halfway into the semester she acknowledged a change of view and growing understanding of those who oppose abortion. This evolution itself deserves analysis, but here I will simply recount one significant conversation we had.

I made some remark about the sexual revolution and how it seemed to me that many young men expected their girlfriends to protect both of them from the consequences of sexual activity, and that thus those men were not only fleeing responsibility but also collaborating in what was a subtle "con" of the woman. I observed it is the woman who gets pregnant and the woman, in most cases, who is expected to use contraceptives—despite their notorious side-effects. And of course it is the woman who must have the abortion, with its frequent lifetime guilt and, often after a second abortion, consequent permanent infertility. The man might be "liberated," I observed, but it seemed the woman is enslaved. By her desire to please him without insisting on a permanent relationship, she yields herself to forces beyond her control. The result is often rejection after years of marriage-without-benefit-of-clergy. The young lady agreed and then noted bitterly: "A girl gets the full treatment in a singles' bar. That's where they look you over as if you're no more than a piece of meat."

She intuitively grasped how dehumanized is the playboy's lust and instinctively shrank from the fleeting tryst in which the only purpose of a woman's beauty is to package something to be devoured by a man's appetites. But I doubt she perceived the continuum among the use, by unmarried persons, of contraceptives, which she found unobjectionable; abortion, the harm of which she was beginning to discern; and the "meat market" style of the swinging singles among her age group.

Yet that continuum is there. The contraceptive mentality makes sex-for-entertainment a possible way of life. With the abortion "backup," a man or woman is "freed" to visit the singles' meat market whenever the urge moves them. But there is a price to pay (besides the rarely mentioned price of venereal disease): the reduction of human love, which must say "Always," to animal lust, which says only "Just now, *not* always." Love wills the good of the other, even to the sacrifice of the self. Lust wills the good of the self, even to the sacrifice of the other. Love must have a spiritual element, for it transcends the passage of time and the fading of beauty. Lust rejects spirit, for it lasts only for the present and it depends only on visible attraction.

Sexual relationships without permanence and without children leave men and women with only *self*-fulfillment as the reason for their involvement. The main spiritual result of contraception/abortion is solipsism—the isolation of the individual self.

In an incisive article, "Marriage and the Rejection of Sacrifice," Donald Demarco details the expansion of the "culture of narcissism" during the 1970s.[1] The "imperial self" who now spends his time "looking out for number one" rejects parenthood even in marriage. Demarco cites the recent deluge of popular books discouraging married couples from having children: such titles as *The Baby Trap*, *The Case Against Having Children*, *Marriage is Hell*, and *Childless by Choice* all urge the same ideology—namely, that husband and wife should think first and foremost of themselves. These books and magazine articles with such titles as, "How Do You Really Feel About Having Children?" and "Do I Want a Baby?" propagandize the view that the modern couple should decide about children by balancing anticipated self-fulfillment against anticipated sacrifice. Crank into the equation dirty diapers and crayon-smudged walls and the cost of college tuition and you have the convenience argument for avoiding parenthood altogether.

But where then does the money go? Nowhere else but to purchase fine things for oneself—travel, lavish entertainments, and the building of one's own holdings in real estate, expensive wines, vintage autos, and collectibles. Personal comfort and convenience, abetted by the technology of mass-produced sterility, becomes the new ethical norm. The reader could name half-a-dozen top television hits, situation comedies and soap operas, in which the wealthy and lustful "beautiful people" give free rein to their passions but hardly ever involve themselves in a traditional family with faithful spouses. Television fiction now takes paganism so much for granted that its heroes and heroines seem purposely to reject biblical principles and do not even acknowledge, in their sin, that those principles make any claim on them. In most cases, the highest value television would teach us is self-gratification. Yet the scripture teaches just the opposite:

> Then Jesus said to his disciples, "If any man will come after me, let him deny himself, take up his cross, and follow me.
> For whosoever will save his life shall lose it; and whosoever will lose his life for my sake shall find it.
> For what does it profit a man, if he shall gain the whole world, and lose his own soul? or what shall a man give in exchange for his soul? (Mt 16:24-26)

The sex-for-entertainment/sex-without-responsibility mentality makes it possible to reject the command to take up one's cross. The family is a school for the parents as well as for the children. Raising children for twenty years till they are adults provides parents endless occasions for patience, cheerfulness, and self-giving. The family is the essential unit of society not merely because of the children's need for permanent adult care, but also because it provides a temporal context for transcendent ends. We must see the profound in the petty, the will of God in a baby's midnight cry; we must learn the mind of Christ.

The Lord was self-disciplined and self-sacrificing. He came that we may have life more abundantly; he came to transfer his life to us, and in the process he "emptied himself." This is exactly what parents do: they empty themselves for their children. Family life requires continual giving. The parent must cut his children's meat at dinner while his own gets cold, he must do those diapers, erase those crayon smudges, pay the doctor's bills, spend sleepless nights because the little person in the next room wheezes with strep throat, make those sandwiches for school lunches, attend those soccer games for half the day, get the kids up early for swim practice and sit up late awaiting the teenagers' return. Writers on the spiritual life state the soul must go through three overlapping stages: the purgative, illuminative, and unitive ways. Family life is filled with joys; but it also provides plenty of occasion for self-purgation, not the least of which is postponing parental gratification for the sake of the children's immediate needs. After first kicking against the goad, the parent comes to realize that the gratifying action, opportunity, trip, TV program, or whatever, is far less important in the divine scheme than being an occasion of grace for his child. Far from being an obstacle to personal fulfillment, children are an occasion of personal fulfillment. They enable an empty person to be filled with Christ. The anti-child mentality prevents the gestation in us of a human child and of Jesus Christ himself. One of the great ironies of the sexual revolution, then, is its two-fold barrenness: those who adopt its disvalues end by being no more than what they were at the beginning—empty people who have given birth to neither natural nor supernatural life.

Pornography: Lust Capitalized

It is hard to discuss pornography with Christians because they are not familiar with it. Their innate good sense prevents them from exposing themselves to its corruption. Consequently they often awaken to the pornography plague only when an "adult bookstore" or X-rated movie or particularly offensive "skin magazine" appears in their area. Then too, many think that mere nudity, which seems relatively innocuous, typifies pornography today. Christians who do not expose themselves to pornography do not know how savage and degrading it is. Their grasp of the problem of perversity in public morals is further confused by the one-sided message from the media that "anything goes" because "freedom of speech" is an absolute which cannot be restrained in our constitutional system.

The bias in public discourse on this topic came home to me in May of 1973 when the University of Cincinnati Law School invited a local A.C.L.U. attorney and me to debate the question of whether there should be some legal controls over obscenity/pornography. My opponent gave an eloquent, though familiar, argument that the First Amendment "required" that there be no laws against pornography, because "a book never corrupted anyone," that there was no harm in looking at dirty pictures, and that the essence of freedom was that one citizen should not impose his morality on another. I had heard it all before; my problem was that students and faculty in the audience had heard it all too. But they had not heard the case for public morality. As the second speaker, I therefore began by asking the members of the audience to raise their hands in response to a couple of questions.

"How many of you have ever heard or read a serious argument *against* legal control of obscenity, such as my opponent has just made?" Out of an audience of 300 people, practically every hand went up.

"How many of you have ever heard or read a serious argument *for* any legal control of obscenity?" Perhaps a dozen hands went up.

"There you have it," I said. "Not only must I rebut my opponent's twenty-minute talk in the same amount of time; I must also rebut a whole lifetime of impressions you have picked up, all on one side of the issue."

This experience reinforced an observation from my teaching. As a professor at Georgetown and later Indiana Law School, I naturally used a constitutional law casebook that included court decisions on obscenity law. I was troubled that the book, like most in the field, did not really tell the students *why* there was any law against obscenity. By the time the Supreme Court started accepting challenges to obscenity laws, the Court seemed to have forgotten the answer too. I had this paradox in mind—that the nation's highest court seemed ignorant of the reasons why it upheld, in principle at least, a body of constitutional rulings—when an unexpected phone call reached my office at Indiana Law School in February of 1977.

"This is a television station in Chicago [naming the station] calling. Can you come up here tomorrow for the taping of a four-man talk show debate on obscenity? We want to have two people on each side, and we understand you are qualified to take the anti-obscenity position."

"Who else will be your guests?" I asked.

"On your side, Bill Berg, who runs his own talk show on another station, WGN Radio. On the other side, Harry Reems and Larry Flynt. Reems played in 'Deep Throat.' Flynt publishes *Hustler* magazine."

I asked how they got my name and why me, since there are six law schools in Chicago, two of which are church-affiliated. One presumes that there should be at least one local law professor who would be willing to debate Mr. Flynt on television. The answer was that no one else whom they had called wanted to do it.

Fearful that the argument would go by default, and a hundred thousand TV viewers in Chicago, like those law students at Cincinnati, would have a lifetime prejudice reinforced by never hearing it challenged, I accepted, with one condition: "Berg and I may not be the attraction for your audience, but if you want a day of my professional time for no stipend, you owe me one concession: we get equal time." Without hesitation, they agreed.

As it turned out, however, they broke the promise of equal

time: Messrs. Reems and Flynt were allowed to argue their case to a sympathetic moderator and audience for eighteen minutes before Mr. Berg and I were invited to come on camera. But the occasion provided me the unwelcome opportunity to glance through *Hustler* magazine just before the show, courtesy of the program producer. It contained photo close-ups of sexual organs in sex acts, ads for child-like dolls that simulated sex acts, interviews with prostitutes, a "cartoon" laughing at child abuse ("Chester the Molester"), and other pictures too debased to mention. My momentary brush with this filth did help rhetorically, in a surprising way, during the program. Mr. Flynt insisted at one point that "You wouldn't want to censor a discussion of sex like this program. Then why do you want to censor *Hustler*?" To which I responded: "If *Hustler* magazine is merely a 'discussion of sex,' like a gynecology text, then let the cameraman focus back there where the producer has a copy; zoom in on the pictures that *Hustler* contains, and give the people of Chicago a close-up. Let *them* decide whether *Hustler* is just a medical text." The reaction to this brazen suggestion was consternation in the glass-walled control booth: hands signaling, No, No, Don't!; grimaces conjuring up angry F.C.C. lawyers; faces anticipating angry phone calls from the audience.

Later, upon reflection, I was irritated at the breached equal time promise and frustrated that the very crudity of pornography prevents one from telling the truth about it to those ignorant of its vileness. Moreover, from the moderator's and audience's sympathies, I realized they too did not know what pornography is or why the nation has tried to control it or what harm it does. To remedy this public ignorance to some extent, I succeeded, in May 1977, in publishing in *The National Observer* newspaper (a now-defunct family-style weekly published by Dow Jones) an "op-ed" piece titled, "A Parent's Case Against Pornography." Numerous reprintings of this article in other periodicals led to an invitation to contribute to a law review symposium on the topic a year later.[2] During the course of writing this article, I learned that in many large cities there are "sex entertainment clubs" where patrons can find private rooms and willing consorts for most of the activities depicted in magazines like *Hustler*; that there are over 260 monthly magazines catering to pedophiles—people who get their kicks from gawking at nude children in compromising poses; there are private clubs of people who use the mails to order and trade pictures of such children; and that the burgeoning cable TV industry offers late-night "adult movies" for hotel and for home.

All this is grim enough; it is grimmer still for Christian citizens. Pornography is self-entertainment by vicarious experience, in imagination, of the sexual activity in the photo or film. The pornophile stimulates himself by entering a fantasy world of sex that completely absorbs his imagination. He performs psychic masturbation; he allows himself to be drawn into the action. The pornographic film is effective, according to its own standards, to the extent that it helps the viewer experience what the actors experienced: unrestrained passion unleased. Pornography is visualized lust.

The social moralist—which group includes but is not limited to Christians—opposes epidemic pornography on numerous grounds. It promotes lust, and lust is essentially selfish. The person given over to lust wants to devour, to cannibalize, the other person, whom he sees as no more than a foil or organ. It destroys the proper delicacy and respect that should exist between men and women. It ennervates the spirit, rendering any real self-sacrifice for higher values such as family or country extremely difficult.

Though crude, pornography is a philosophical statement. It says: there are no rules about sex; sex is trivial; sex is for entertainment. Though debased, pornography is a theological statement. It says: there is no God who says I should limit my lust or channel my passion or give as well as get. Though preoccupied with sex, pornography is anti-woman and anti-child. It is anti-marriage and anti-permanence. Thus it is profoundly anti-civilization. Since civilization is social support to the dynamics of life, pornography is anti-life.

The Christian recognizes pornography as spiritual death. It

lets a person sin without having a sinful consort physically with him. It is the perverse mirror-reversal of prayer: in prayer the spiritual man can "go elsewhere" and do good to others through the power of God; in pornography the carnal man can "go elsewhere" and do evil with others through the power of lustful fantasy.

This perversity of personality is so pervasive that even when the man is not sinning sexually he is locked inside his own ego, where, because he lacks existence of his own, he is truly empty. He is locked inside an empty room as long as he pursues fantasies God commands he avoid. This psychic solitude is the antechamber to hell. And the "mercy" of Satan is not as kindly as a ravenous lion falling upon a baby deer.

To grasp the connection between pornography and its brutalizing effects, the Christian has to realize how predatory and animalistic it is. The modern forms of pornography include, in livid color, zoom-lens close-ups of women having intercourse with dogs and horses, lesbian masturbation, techniques of rape, heterosexual and homosexual masturbation, methods of seducing and molesting children, group sex acts, fetishistic ways to stimulate oneself, close-ups of sex organs in aroused state, and "snuff films" in which a person is attacked sexually and then actually murdered before the camera.

Immersion in images of such actions destroys psychic balance, for it severs one's grip on reality and teaches distortions about relationships with the opposite sex and about exclusivity in marriage. Pornography teaches a man that a woman is no more than an outlet for his passions, that the act is more important than the person joining in it, that pleasure is the only purpose, and that there are no rules or restrictions from God or nature that might channel his passions or lead to the conception of children. Pornography sometimes disposes to rape, sexual assault, child molestation. It always destroys the moral fiber through the accumulation of impressions sinking into the subconscious and warping the moral sense. The psychiatrist Dr. Frederic Wertham, in an article titled

"Medicine and Mayhem," said this about psychiatric disorders caused by films of violent sex:

> With regard to sex, the explicit display of sadomasochistic scenes may have lasting effects. They may supply the first suggestions for special forms or reinforce existing tendencies. The whole orientation of young people with regard to the dignity of women is affected. By showing cruelty with erotic overtones, we teach that there can be pleasure in inflicting pain on others.[3]

The harm to society as a whole is as tragic as the harm to the individual. Pornography promotes a lifestyle of radical selfishness. This attitude, spreading among thousands and perhaps millions of young men and not a few young women, will spill over from their private lives onto the social, moral, and political life of society as a whole. It contributes to impermanent relationships, the "living together" arrangement among perhaps a million couples, and the heightened frequency of divorce.

I do not suggest that pornography is at the heart of all these developments in every case. But it contributes to the aggressive selfishness of our age, and because it is a lie about love, marriage, sex, parenthood, and self-giving, it perverts actions and relationships at the center of social life. Its spread is an index of our culture's moral collapse. Worse still, the indifference of Christians to pornography suggests that their priests and ministers do not read the scriptures carefully on this point, nor do they reflect deeply on the importance of public morality and the need to strengthen spiritual and self-sacrifice of a people.

The law has always held that pornography is not "protected speech." That is, the ordinary constitutional protections for freedom of speech do not apply to obscenity and pornography because these overlapping genres of perversion simply are not speech. Or, to state the Supreme Court's position differently, but to emerge with the same conclusion: some kinds of speech—libel, defamation, "fighting words," obscenity/pornography—are not protected by the Constitution. Therefore, the law may make the production or distribution of such pseudo-speech criminal and prosecute those who traffic in it. This has always been the state of the law, in theory; and it is the state of our law today.[4]

Why then is there so much pornography, or near-pornography, on our bookstands; so much outright pornography in the ubiquituous "adult" bookstores, so much blatant pornography on certain segments of cable TV and in numerous downtown movie houses? Why indeed, when every poll shows that at least seventy percent of the people want stronger laws against pornography, especially against the perversity of "kiddie porn."

The answer is that we do not enforce the laws we have. Every state has anti-pornography laws, most cities and counties have comparable laws, and there are numerous federal statutes dealing with the use of the mails to transmit pornography, trafficking in minors for pornographic purposes, and other elements of the pandering of pornographic depictions. But prosecutors are slow to bring cases. First, their budgets are limited, and they often feel little public pressure or support to expend time and energy on nonviolent crimes when so many violent crimes need their attention. Second, local prosecutors' relatively young legal staffs are often outgunned by pornographers' experienced and highly paid defense counsel. It is embarrassing to take hundreds of hours of an attorney's time only to have some subtle technical fault in their pleading or practice trigger an appellate court reversal of a conviction. Third, prosecutors are reluctant because even convictions which "stick" sometimes carry with them only slap-on-the-wrist penalties by permissive judges who themselves lack a moral sense of outrage at the debasement widespread pornography is spreading in society.

I witnessed a classic illustration of these flaws in our legal approach to pornography in Virginia when the state attempted to prosecute a particularly outrageous "adult bookstore" for pandering a dozen different films of sexual perversion. I sat in at the all-day trial on six felony counts, viewed the films when the jury did, and observed the examination and cross-examination of witnesses. The young prosecutor, who had no funds to pay for the services of an "expert witness," dueled with three defense counsel, the senior of whom may well have earned as much for his work on this one trial as the prosecutor earned in a year. The defense team engaged a "professor of sexuality" from a local university, as an "expert," to testify that watching other people on film performing acts of sexual intercourse was not "prurient." They also commissioned a costly telephone poll of a random sample of the residents of Fairfax County purporting to show that explicit sexual entertainments were acceptable "community standards."

Despite his lack of experience and lack of financial resources to build a professional case, this prosecutor obtained convictions from the jury on all the felony counts—for the films, which the jury watched in the courtroom, were indeed obscene and they spoke for themselves to people of some common sense. But the judge, whose rulings from the bench clearly indicated his annoyance that his time was taken up in a trial on such a subject, fined the defendants a mere $950 on each count. The defendants, the manager, and the clerk of the so-called bookstore, were themselves only pawns in a much bigger chessgame; probably the syndicate which controlled their product paid the fine out of profits as a cost of doing business. Had the defendants gone to jail, it would not have been for long and, in any event, would not have given the kingpins controlling the distribution system the slightest moment's pause.

Until Christians and other Americans concerned about the collapse of public morality organize to influence prosecutors to bring more cases, judges to give stiffer punishments, and legislatures to pass laws with sharper "teeth," the porn shops will remain open and the stuff will spread closer and closer to our homes through television and movies.[5]

Sex Education: Twisting the Twig

In the spring of 1977, I chanced to see a Public Television documentary on public school "sex education." The program focused on a high school in Fairfax County, Virginia, a largely upper-middle-class suburb of Washington, D.C. I watched with great interest because I planned to relocate my family to the Washington area in a few months.

Two scenes were striking. The first was a mixed classroom of adolescent boys and girls where the teacher had filled the blackboard with drawings of various contraceptive devices such as foam, condoms, IUDs, and the pill to stimulate class discussion. The second scene was a separate interview with the teacher, who kept insisting that "We don't teach values, we teach techniques. It's for the home and the church to teach values."

Most if not all of the children were unmarried. The classroom approach was indifferent to questions of right and wrong. The teacher believed that "being sexually active" was matter of subjective taste and preference, like preferring chocolate ice cream over vanilla. Parents supposedly were not able to "talk about sex." Supposedly the children were all on the same sophisticated level and felt no embarrassment at such intimate discussion matters as what condom to use or the relation between penis and vagina.

Though the teacher claimed the school did not teach values, it had the advantage over home and church. The school put its prestige behind a repeated program (complete with films and written assignments) with "certified" teachers who were "experts." In 1977, the sex ed curriculum did not go into "alternative lifestyles" or abortion. But by 1981, masturbation, homosexuality, lesbianism, and abortion were under serious consideration for inclusion in a revised curriculum.

Early in the 1970s religious-liberty attorney William Ball represented some Baptist parents in Michigan who sued the local school board over the grammar school mandatory sex education program.[6] They demonstrated the program's relativism, agnosticism, and permissive experimentation limited only by the warning, "Don't get caught!" (i.e., pregnant). They noted that the schools silently inculcated these values without open debate. They observed that attitudes resembling those of the Humanist Manifesto were taught but that Bible-based views of sex did not receive "equal time."

When atheist children complained, twenty years ago, of having to be present in school when a short prayer was recited, the prayer was dropped. The Baptist parents argued that if peer group pressure made true voluntariness impossible in the prayer case, *a fortiori* it was impossible in the sex ed case. The prayer is brief, the children distracted, the prayer hardly ever is discussed after school. The sex course is long, the children attentive, it is the after-hours preoccupation of most of the students. The norms of conduct taught in the school were directly contrary to the Bible-based norms the parents were trying to teach at home. Since the parental values arose out of their Christian religion, the state schools were infringing on their religious free exercise by promoting a different set of values; and by promoting a viewpoint central to secular humanism, were, they argued, "establishing" it as the religion of the schools.[7]

One can argue whether these parents were trying to prove too much, but some aspects of the question are beyond cavil. One is that there is no evidence that sex education discourages adolescent sexual activity; for knowledge does not equal virtue, and information about how to do something pleasurable rarely motivates a person *not* to do it. Again, children mature at different rates; what might be psychologically acceptable for one child can be inappropriate and even harmful for another. Then too, sex education is simply unsuited for a *group* of thirty fifteen-year-old boys and girls.[8]

Because the question of being "sexually active"—the modern euphemism for "promiscuous"—is at root a question whether it is *right or wrong* to be sexually active, it is utterly impossible to divorce technique from morality. Whether or not it is "establishing the religion of secular humanism," sex education surely does take a stand on moral issues—usually without equal time for rebuttal. As a vehicle for moral attitudes it is powerful; unlike discussions of Lincoln's honesty or Teddy Roosevelt's courage, sex education engages the emotions as well as the mind, and can be carried out easily in practice after school.[9]

Sex education is part of the sexual revolution. As such, it resembles many modern political revolutions. On the surface, it is apparently a "spontaneous combustion" of natural forces catching fire because of chemical or atmospheric conditions. Actually the revolution is the planned promotion of a small group of dedicated activists who privately forge the "necessary conditions" and then publically take advantage of what they themselves helped create.[10]

Sex education for children up to twelfth grade is supposedly the path to mental and physical health. Supposedly young people will not "get in trouble" as often if they know the techniques and the consequences. But the sex educators assume that "trouble" is a physical/intellectual matter and not a matter of virtue and values. They also think that since knowledge is good, more knowledge is better, a view contrary to the traditional wisdom that it is not good for parents to share everything with children and that a public group is not the time and place for discussing intimacies. One does not teach would-be arsonists how to make bombs.[11]

"When the blind lead the blind, both shall fall into the pit." It appears that most sex educators cannot answer the essential first question: what *is* psychological/moral health? Just as a good doctor must know what normal health is if he would treat disease in the human body, so the "educator" who would teach how to avoid the "wrong" way to handle sex must have an ideal of what is the "right" way to handle it.

Many psychologists now question whether grammar school children should deal with sex at all. They have come to understand the importance of the integrity of the "latency period." This is the time of life when the child normally renounces what Freud called his "oedipal strivings" and represses from conscious memory his early experiences of childhood longing and attraction to the parent of the opposite sex. As Dr. Rhoda L. Lorand, a clinical psychoanalyst and author of the bestselling book *Sex and the Teenager* has written, with the onset of the latency period

> the child quiets down and turns his attention to achievements which lead him into the grownup world. The sexual passions and interests of those early years go underground for the most part. . . . The child then becomes educable. All his energy and interests are channeled into learning concrete subjects, skills and hobbies. The learning process, Freud discovered, works with the sublimated sexual curiosity, sublimated sexual energy, and the sublimated aggressive instinct.[12]

In an essay comparing the anthropological immaturity of primitive people with the psychological immaturity characteristic of youngsters whose latency period has been prematurely ruptured, psychiatrist Dr. Melvin Anchell describes the latency period as follows:

> The natural re-direction of the sexual energies is manifested in the intense capacity and desire for learning characteristic of this period of transition between childhood and adolescence. Usually occurring between the ages of six and thirteen, it is known as the "latency period," because the sexual drive *per se* remains dormant or latent. School children of this age are generally indifferent or asexual in their attitude toward their peers of the opposite sex. They are inherently preoccupied with their own individual development and needs which are devoid of direct sexual aims. Subconscious sexual urges are released in fantasies and dreams.[13]

Yet sex education courses typically begin in the middle years of elementary school and some begin in first grade. They infect the curriculum under such headings as Family Planning;

Health, Biology, Life Sciences; Social Science; Human Sexuality; and even Home Economics. In first grade, sex ed may start with a "mixed-group" tour of bathrooms and an explanation of male and female genital parts. By fourth grade, many students receive a detailed description of sexual intercourse.[14]

Whatever the theory of "morally neutral" sex education—at root, impossible, because issues of life's purpose and morality are central—the practice of sex education invariably is covertly un-Christian.[15] Sometimes it is overtly anti-Christian.

Thus, on sexual conduct the Bible teaches: "Therefore a man leaves his father and his mother and cleaves to his wife, and they become one flesh (Gn 2:24; Mt 19:5). And Paul asks, "Do you not know that he who joins himself to a prostitute becomes one body with her? For, as it is written, 'The two shall become one'" (1 Cor 6:16). Yet a Planned Parenthood booklet tells teenagers: "Sex is fun and joyful, courting is fun and joyful, and it comes in all types and styles, all of which are okay. Do what gives pleasure and enjoy what gives pleasure, and ask for what gives pleasure. Don't rob yourself of joy by focusing on old-fashioned ideas about what's 'normal' or 'nice.'"

On moral values, the scriptures tell us to "have this mind among yourselves, which you have in Christ Jesus" (Phil 2:5), "have a clear conscience toward God and toward men" (Acts 24:16), "put on the Lord Jesus Christ, and make no provision for the flesh, to gratify its desires" (Rom 13:14), and "cleanse ourselves from every defilement of body and spirit" (2 Cor 7:1). Yet a widely used sex education book, *Sexuality and the School*, by Marianne and Sidney Simon, states that parents with traditional values are intolerant, ignorant, and bigoted; that sex educators approach such matters as sex outside marriage, homosexuality, masturbation, abortion, contraception, and incest with "openness" so as to "relieve" the child's anxieties; and urges different values to supplant the old "immorality of morality."

On the role of parents and the family, the Bible teaches us to "train up the child in the way he should go" so that "when he is old he will not depart from it" (Prv 22:6); to teach children the

Lord's commandments (Dt 11:19); and Paul directs fathers to "bring them [children] up in the discipline and instruction of the Lord" (Eph 6:4). But many sex education texts denigrate the parents. They suggest that parents are mean, lack sensitivity, and hold foolish and old-fashioned values. Despite the commandment to "honor thy father and thy mother," the sex education texts teach that no religious views are to deflect the child from self-gratification and self-assertion. Though the parents teach objective values, sex ed courses urge "experimental lifestyles" and situational values.

The scriptures condemn adultery, lust, fornication, uncleanness, lasciviousness so many times that direct quote is not necessary. (See Gal 5:19-21; 1 Pt 2:11; 1 Thes 5:22; Ex 20:14; Mt 5:27; Prv 6:20-35; Acts 15:20 and 21:25.) But sex education teaches that we need not sublimate the carnal nature and that narcissistic self-gratification is the shortcut to "self-fulfillment." For the sex educator, what people do is equivalent to what they ought to do. He has no norm to guide the children, and he is fascinated with sexual deviations. Very few sex educators would disagree with this statement from *Humanist Manifesto II* (1973):

> . . . the many varieties of sexual exploration should not in themselves be considered evil. . . . Individuals should be permitted to express their sexual proclivities and pursue their life-style as desired.

I do not know whether preoccupation with the perverse is due to subconscious desire to justify one's private inclinations, or whether it is no more than an expression of thoughtless enthusiasm for "change" coupled with the liberal/radical's usual resentment of tradition, rules, and Christian teaching. My hunch is that considerable sexual experimentation takes place among the professional "sex educators"; most "true believers" in a reformist creed tend to practice what they preach. But whether the sex educators "do it" is really secondary; they *are* teaching our children to "do it."[16] Christians must remember that this movement is a crusade to make the world better by substituting one set of values for another. Instead of "Blessed are the pure of heart," the children now hear "Gratified are the impure of action."

Christians should do everything possible to keep this kind of sex education away from their children. They should question the credentials of the sex education teachers. They should examine the textbooks. Some should insist that their children be excused. If they cannot, then they should demand "equal time" for spokesmen for Christian self-control. When told that parents don't teach their children enough about sex, they should demand sex education for parents in return for dropping student sex education.

Once again, because the Christians were passive while secular humanists were active, the legal situation is not favorable. Politically, public school administrators are remote and not subject to direct parental supervision; school boards are busy about many things and in large districts it is especially difficult to influence their decisions on curriculum. Legally, in many states it is difficult to exempt one's children from mandatory sex education classes without the expense and trauma of a lawsuit. Even if they could be excused, many children will have to possess the courage of early Christian martyrs to resist the peer group harassment sure to be leveled at the "prudes" and "squares" who absent themselves from a hot subject like sex ed. Another possibility is to insist on "equal time" for Christian sexual principles offered within the course as an alternative to the humanistic relativism. This request is unlikely to be granted, but the very request, if made insistently and in terms of elemental fairness, should caution the curriculum experts that Christian parents will resist the more blatant propaganda for promiscuity and deviance.

Homosexual/Lesbian Practice

At the very beginning of the scripture we are told, "God created man in his own image, in the image of God created he him; male and female created he them" (Gn 1:27). God commanded man to "leave his father and mother and cleave unto his wife" (Gn 2:24). And the passages in Genesis dealing with Sodom make clear how outraged God is by homosexual practice. In the epistle of Jude, that Apostle states bluntly:

> And the angels that did not keep their own position but left their proper dwelling have been kept by him in eternal chains in the nether gloom until the judgment of the great day; just as Sodom and Gomorrah and the surrounding cities, which likewise acted immorally and indulged in unnatural lust, serve as an example by undergoing a punishment of eternal fire.
>
> Yet in like manner these men in their dreamings defile the flesh, reject authority, and revile the glorious ones. (6-8)

And Peter teaches the identical doctrine:

> God did not spare the angels when they sinned, but cast them into hell . . . by turning the cities of Sodom and Gomorrah to ashes he condemned them to extinction and made them an example to those who were to be ungodly; and . . . he rescued righteous Lot, greatly distressed by the licentiousness of the wicked. (2 Pt 2:4, 7)

Words like "preference" and "orientation" dilute this uncompromising teaching. The *sin* does not lie in a man's *inclination*; it lies in his *choice,* in his deliberate act. There is too much gushy sentimentality about this question. No serious Christian who has taken on the mind of Christ about fallen human nature should feel hostility toward *any* group of people. The Lord is merciful and forgiving and so should his followers be. But at the same time, the condition of mercy and forgiveness is repentance and firm purpose of amendment. It follows that Christians should stand up to the media propaganda that they are "discriminating" against a "minority group." Christians must understand that the issue is *not* one of private "orientation," but it is one of *actions*. For homosexual sins, these actions necessitate a consort, a need which often entails recruitment from the heterosexual majority, and sometimes recruitment of children and teenagers unprepared to make a truly mature decision "between consenting adults in private," as even the secular humanists say sexual choice should be. Nor are homosexuals a civil rights "minority"; it turns democracy upside down to require the majority of society to give special favors to people whose conduct offends community moral standards. Yet the movement to amend civil rights laws to add homosexuals to the groups who historically have suffered irrational discrimination insists that the violators of public decency standards be rewarded. Then too, since the sinner's repentance is the condition for forgiveness, Christians are not obligated to welcome back into the Christian community any person, homosexual or heterosexual, who insists on violating God's laws for sexual conduct. To do so would be to disregard God's law by pretending it does not matter whether one lives a sinful or sinless life. Whether reconciliation with the larger Christian community or legal treatment in secular society is the question, Christians must remember that *private sympathy for the individual sinner is quite different from public encouragement for a deviant group*.

The law is a general norm of conduct. It expresses the majority's moral norms to guide the ignorant, protect the unwary, and set the public moral tone of social decency. By a legal policy that excludes practicing homosexuals from school teaching, for instance, Christians do not "impose their morality" on non-Christians any more than a policy of "affirmative action" to hire such persons imposes non-Christian (im)morality on Christians. The law is not neutral on values. The question is, Whose values?

The gay rights movement seeks to use law in three interrelated ways, all of which pursue a privileged status for homosexual activity. First, the movement tries to persuade courts to deem private actions excluding homosexual individuals from some opportunity or employment to be "discrimination," a word which connotes a wrongful (because arbitrary and irrational) bias against a person who has a right to be treated "equally." Thus a Christian church in San Francisco, which had unwittingly hired a homosexual to be its organist, was the target of such a lawsuit when he was dismissed. The aggrieved individual was asking an arm of government, a civil court, to evaluate the inner moral position of a private religious body and to decide that it could not act on those moral convictions to maintain its own spiritual integrity. Though one may sympathize with the discomfort of the individual, to permit courts to reconstruct the ethical imperatives of a Christian church in accord with secular presumptions about what is "right," "natural," or "good sexual conduct" is to secularize the church at its very core. Fortunately, in this case, the trial court recognized the church's constitutional free exercise of religion and did not attempt to meddle in its internal moral discipline.

Second, the gay rights movement seeks to use regulatory rules, a species of law, to the same end. For example, state housing authorities are beginning to issue rules affecting the decisions of landlords whose apartment buildings come under governmental policies because their financing arrangements are subsidized. The rules in question sometimes prohibit refusal to rent to would-be tenants because of their "sexual preference" or "sexual status." That is, a landlord might have to rent to two or more known homosexual tenants, despite his personal religious convictions and his desire not to promote a "lifestyle" which he and his other tenants deem a terribly unbiblical example for their children. Once again, the law, or law-sanctioned bureaucratic rules, can become a device to destroy community norms and to prevent a person who supports the Judeo-Christian ethic from using his own property in a way consonant with his religious and moral beliefs. Further, such rules undermine the landlord's ability to raise his children in biblical principles if they prevent him from excluding tenants who flaunt a lifestyle hostile to his religious values. And by placing the onus of illegality on his shoulders rather than on the tenants', the regulation will transfer the opprobrium from those who reject traditional morality to those who would preserve it.

Third, the episodic activities I have described in the last two paragraphs will receive new impetus if the Congress passes some of the bills before it which would insert "sexual orientation" or "sexual preference" into the various civil rights laws. For to refuse known homosexuals certain housing, teaching assignments, and employment opportunities in public and private groups, one would be violating civil rights laws just as he would if he refused these things to blacks because of their race or women because of their sex. Since the average person does not have the time, energy, resources, or heart for a prolonged and costly lawsuit, many will surely capitulate to the real or anticipated attack through courts and regulatory bodies. The next step would likely be "affirmative action" for homosexuals, a euphemistic phrase meaning *de facto* pursuit of quotas for the "minority" group. Then the power of government, with its ability to dangle the carrot of funding or wave the stick of possible penalties for resistance, will be brought to bear on housing projects, schools, universities, neighborhoods, corporations, and other organizations within the long reach of the law, to force them to seek out, hire, and promote, the "exploited minority"—the homosexuals.

One does not want to cry "Wolf!" when there is no wolf present. At the same time, silence is dangerous when one sees wolf tracks in the snow outside. The problem of homosexual status and homosexual practice is a difficult one; but it will not be solved by Christian capitulation to a movement to treat as normal and deserving of almost compensatory governmental efforts a "lifestyle" which the Bible condemns.

The State: Big Brother to the Revolution

In the twentieth century, revolutionaries strive to capture the state and then use its power, from laws to budgets, to promote a New Order. The promoters of a new pagan ideal of sex have followed this course as well. Negatively, they have largely succeeded in gutting the laws against pornography so that the definitions of adult pornography are difficult and enforcement of the law spotty. They have also succeeded in driving out of public school education any institutional reference to Christian moral values. Affirmatively, they are already funding numerous Planned Parenthood "clinics" and programs, all teaching that "being sexually active" is quite all right as long as one uses contraceptives. Moves are afoot to rewrite "civil rights laws" to give homosexuals preferential treatment. Moreover, they have quietly revised most state laws to enable them to insert themselves between the parents and their children, a remarkable and ominous accomplishment which was brought home to me by this actual experience.

In the early 1970s I was asked by a group of parents in Northfield, Illinois, to represent them at a public hearing one evening at the local town hall. The topic was the medical and psychological services to be offered at a new "health clinic" to be set up, with state funds, near the local public high school. The enabling legislation, signed by then-Governor Ogilvie, authorized "health care professionals," "psychological counselors," and "social workers," along with physicians, to provide a range of care and medical advice on such matters as drug use, neurosis, pregnancy and how to avoid it, abortion, venereal disease, and all the other "hygiene" problems afflicting minors. The statute expressly stated that such persons could provide information, counseling, and medicines or medical devices *without the parents' consent and even without their knowledge.* The panelists at the public hearing that night were a school spokesman and two female representatives of Planned Parenthood. Northfield, like neighboring Northbrook, where I then resided, are relatively affluent, upper-middle-class suburbs, where the residents have a high level of educational training, family cohesiveness, financial resources, and interest in their children's well-being.

To ensure there would be a permanent record of the presentation and responses to citizen questions, I engaged a professional court reporter to make a transcript. However, the chairman of the meeting, the city manager, insisted I could not keep a stenographic record, even though I offered to allow the speakers to "revise and extend" their off-the-cuff remarks to make sure that the transcript accurately reflected what they wanted to say. This refusal was especially galling in light of the "public hearing" nature of the meeting, the importance of the topic, and the fact that of the 5,000 or so residents of the township only about 50 were at the meeting. The rest could learn of it only through a transcript printed in the local paper.

But the central point is the exchange I had with Planned Parenthood spokesmen in the course of the meeting. It went along these lines:

"If I wrote you a letter directing that no 'counseling' or medical services be provided my thirteen-year-old daughter, would you honor my request?"

"No."

"If I wrote asking to be notified of what you were doing, would you honor that request?"

"No."

"Would your clinic's physician confer with the family doctor before prescribing medication or, say, birth-control pills for my daughter?"

"No, he would not."

"Why not?"

"Because the family doctor would communicate to you, the parent, the fact that your daughter was using our clinic's services."

"Why is that so bad?"

"Because there is a 'generation gap' between parents and children, and many children are fearful of what their parents would think, and many would not avail themselves of our services if they thought their parents knew."

"You realize, do you not, that as the father of this thirteen-year-old, I have the legal and moral responsibility to care for her, and have been doing just that since the day she was born, and that I care deeply what sort of 'counseling' or medical advice strangers give her?"

"That may be true in your case, but the principle is that the patient-to-physician relationship is sacrosanct, for minors as well as for adults, and parents should not interfere with it."

"What if your clinic fails to obtain from her a complete medical history, and what if you prescribe a medication which is 'contra-indicated,' and what if during a vacation trip to the West Coast my daughter gets sick because of the medication your clinic has provided but I do not know about, and I have to hospitalize her. Would your clinic undertake to pay my medical bills or acknowledge malpractice responsibility?"

The answer was along the lines that this is an unlikely eventuality, that their doctors are careful professionals, and in any event they would have to deal with such a hypothetical case when it actually came up. In other words, they evaded the issue. I turned to the question of moral guidance.

"If a teenage girl comes to you, unmarried and pregnant, would you counsel her to have an abortion?"

"We would lay out for her all possible courses of conduct to remedy the situation."

"Do you realize that for many persons, myself included, abortion is the deliberate taking of innocent human life and is never justified in the hypothetical I have posed?"

"We do not take a stand on moral issues. That is outside our scope. That is for the home or the church. We deal with the medical options. Abortion is one of those options."

"But you just told me that you would not let me know when you were presenting these 'options,' some of which are immoral, to my emotionally burdened, immature minor daughter. How can 'the home or the church' take a stand when it does not know the question is urgent for this child and when your consistent practice is to encourage the child to disguise and hide from the parents at home the fact that you are endorsing a course of conduct which they condemn?"

"I think we should take questions from other people here. You have monopolized the discussion long enough. It is obvious that your attitudes are what gives rise to the need for a clinic such as ours. . . ."

Christians must dispel their distractions about party labels, about so-called "bread-and-butter" issues such as wages and interest rates, and begin to look for and support those candidates for office who will fight Big Brother's efforts to revolutionize our sexual morals, ruin our families, and capture our children's souls.

SEVEN

Exorcising the Spirit of the Age

"For what does it profit a man, if he gains the whole world and forfeits his life?"
—Matthew 16:26

THERE ARE TWO BASIC WAYS to improve human life: change the environment, which presumably makes people better, or change people and they will make their environment better. Secular humanists try to change the environment; Christians must change people's hearts. Those who would change externals can rely upon their own powers and abilities; those who would change men's hearts must rely only on God, for to rely on human skills would be to misconceive the essence of man's problem and make it worse than before.

At once we see that the phrase "to improve human life" hides the core question: "improve" compared to what? Improve for what purpose? Improve in what way? The world has one set of answers to these questions. It wants to raise the standard of living, prolong human life, reduce conflict in the world through international negotiation, redistribute wealth, promote mental health, reduce population growth, make literacy universal, give people unrestricted freedom, render war unlikely if not impossible through disarmament, and expand the reign of justice. Most of these goals seem, on the surface, unobjectionable; indeed, they are desirable. Most Christians would readily endorse these purposes, except for the item demanding unrestricted freedom. Even in this case, quite a few Christians would align themselves with those who disdain past Puritanism and rejoice in "candor," "maturity," "adult freedom," and other shorthand expressions for libertine morality.

Yet the Christian must dissent from the popular wisdom of human self-improvement. Though the litany of collective betterment just recited does itemize, in most cases, social or economic or intellectual improvements for the generality of men and women, the Christian has a different answer to the question "what does it mean to improve human life?" Though socioeconomic improvements are "good," they are not the ultimate Good; to the degree that they distract from the ultimate Good, they indeed may well be evil. For the Christian, good in this world cannot be merely a change of wealth or status, an extension of literacy or longevity, a distribution of food or clothing or shelter. Good is more than worldly comfort. The Christian must ask himself: what does it profit a man if he improve the whole world, and suffer the loss of his immortal soul?

Our predicament is subtle and paradoxical. *The great danger to Christians in the Western countries is not that the ascendant secular humanists are bad men and women, but that by and large they are good men and women.* Unlike the tyrants of history, the evil kings, the conquering generals, and the master criminals who pursued recognizable evil on a grand and mighty scale, the secular humanists in our universities, law firms, television networks, legislatures, and regulatory bodies are good men and women who want to make the world better. They have a vision of progress. They desire human perfection. In many cases their program has some value. They want more Christians to make common cause with them. Many Christians, who would be wary if called to enter an arena with lions, do not hesitate to sit down with agnostics—*not* to discuss God's love, personal spiritual improvement, or conversion to Jesus Christ—but rather how to improve the economy or end censorship or reduce taxes.

Indeed, many influential and thoughtful Christians act as if they are called to do nothing more than baptize the secularist agenda. There are Christian journals whose editorial policy is to promote little more than the "modernization" of the church, the redistribution of wealth, disarmament, and other items on a secular agenda. There are clerics who preach that the "good news of Christ Jesus" virtually mandates Christian suport for complicated and controversial domestic policies. In one sermon I heard shortly before Christmas on the Gospel text narrating John the Baptist's ministry preparing for Jesus' coming, the preacher declared that the modern application of this text was the pursuit of "justice" in this world—specifically, increasing taxes for more government social programs. During the last two years, to point to another example, the most publicized pastoral initiative from America's Catholic bishops was to make recommendations about the nation's nuclear defenses which many thought would weaken these defenses if ever implemented.

One's doubts about these political platforms go far beyond questioning their intrinsic wisdom on political, economic, or strategic grounds. It is true that most Christians who campaign for redistribution of wealth do not know much about economic theory or business practice, but this is not the essential difficulty. It might be argued as well that the Christian campaigners for "justice" place inordinate confidence in the power of government to help the poor and remedy social evils, but this is not the basic objection either. And it is a fact that history shows, as recently as the 1930s, the naivete of unilateral disarmament, but the problem is far deeper than this. To get at the real problem, let us ask the question: how much should the evangelical Christian, whether he be Protestant or Catholic, invest himself in the agenda of politics and economics, even if the agenda were realizable and undoubtedly wise? What if we could truly make the world better by some group's socio-economic program? Should it be the focus of the Christian's energy, the total of his activities, even the object of his prayers? In other words, is the Christian to leap upon the world-improvement bandwagon because, after all, it is "going in the right direction"? Does the Christian have no more to offer the world than a blessing upon the humanists' political and social programs? Is the Christian's influence on the secular humanist agenda to be no more than the chaplain's influence on Congress: open the session with a prayer, as ritual obeisance to bygone beliefs, and then step aside so that the pragmatist power brokers can roll up their sleeves and make things happen?

The basic objection to the Christian's making common cause with the secular humanists is not merely the questionable wisdom of many of their practical methods. Nor is the objection rooted in a denial of the "goodness" of most of their goals. It really lies in the unstated premises of the collaboration: that the Christian is to promote undifferentiated "good" wherever he finds it; that there is a way to bring about the Kingdom of God in this world through human effort; that once we are "in the church" we may continue to do pretty much what we have always done; and that a telling measure of our success as Christians is the accomplishment of economic/social/military "betterment" in this world. The assumption is that the good Christian and the good secularist are working for the same thing. It is a social policy equivalent to the dubious theological claim that "we all worship the same God" and "we are all going to the same goal"—though, of course, "in different ways."

I suggest that we do *not* "all worship the same God." The Christian assents to Christ's exclusive claims:

> *I* am *the* way, the truth, and the life; *no* one comes to the Father, but by me. (Jn 14:6)

> And this is the testimony, that God gave us eternal life, and this life is his Son. He who has the Son has life; *he who has not the Son has not life.* (1 Jn 5:11-12)

We *cannot* all be "going to the same goal but in different ways" because different ways lead to different places. The way of Christians is Jesus, who is *not* the way of those who reject him; and the life in Christians is a life *different* from the life in all others. Neither can we all be "working for the same thing" in social policy. For the humanist, these things are central; for the Christian, these things are nothing unless done in and through and by Jesus.

> I am the vine, you are the branches. He who abides in me, and I in him, he it is that bears much fruit, for *apart from me you can do nothing.* (Jn 15:5)

There is much that is naturally good in the secular agenda, but if the Christian works to achieve it he must do so with a different spirit than the secular humanist who has chosen to "go it alone," without the Spirit of Jesus. The Christian must do it because he "abides" in Jesus and Jesus in him; he must act with and in the Spirit of Jesus. The point is that the Christian's mind is fundamentally different from the secular humanist's even when they work together on the same project. When the secularist does it, it is a man acting; when the Christian does it, it is Jesus-acting-through-a-man. The nearest collaboration of the two can take place in the physical act of person-to-person charity: the "corporal works of mercy," feeding the hungry, clothing the naked, visiting the sick. But when the Christian is inducted into a political cause, he must be wary. For there takes place a subtle shift of emphasis—from helping persons to changing systems. These systems invariably express themselves in worldly terms—budgets, power centers, laws—and subtly erode the spiritual sense, replacing it with the language and symbol and mindset of politics and agitation. This shift contradicts the spirit of the Gospel:

> *My kingship is not of this world*; if my kingship were of this world, my servants would fight . . . but my kingdom is not from the world. (Jn 18:36)

The subtle shift from personal repentance, inner conversion, and the primacy of prayer over to social change, public law, and the primacy of activism betokens a kind of reverse-baptism, a transformation from believer to unbeliever. It is an apostasy from first principles. The touchstone of this apostasy is the reduced place of prayer in the life of the nominal Christian. As he occupies his mind with meetings, speeches, legislative conferences, letter-writing campaigns, study groups, and the other paraphernalia of public policy influence, he loses time for private devotion, liturgy, or scripture study. They can even appear as distractions; after all, the nonbeliever at the disarmament conference, the agnostic planning a public relations strategy for a tax bill, sit shoulder to shoulder with him. They too are eloquent, dedicated, clever, generous with their time; clearly *they* do not take time out for prayer, and yet look how committed, how effective they are!

Claes G. Ryn, the brilliant political theorist, dwelled on this point in a paper delivered in late 1981 at Catholic University to a small group of scholars studying the papal encyclical *Laborem Exercens*. His insight into the problem we are discussing is especially perceptive:

Those today who speak the most and the loudest about the plight of the disadvantaged and about the need to reform society tend to exhibit a generalized caring for nobody in particular. These lovers of humanity take great pride in their own elevated moral sentiments and expect our applause for being the conscience of the world. In righteous indignation they decry the meanness of those who do not share their views of what moral responsibility demands. And because the *language* of their sentiments is often that of Christian love and charity, the essential difference is easily overlooked. It is not noticed, for example, that the humanitarian sympathy on which so many modern people base their claim to moral worth has few, if any, prerequisites of moral character. In the classical and Judaeo-Christian tradition of ethics, love and charity are understood to be the fruits of long and sometimes difficult improvement of self. The great appeal of modern sentimental brotherhood, by contrast, is that it relieves man of moral effort. Nothing is easier than caring in the abstract for the suffering poor, or the exploited proletariat, or the starving Third World. Indeed, a merely sentimental caring has the advantage of somehow always transferring real obligations to some agency other than oneself, such as government or an international organization. It is quite possible to bask in self-approbation for one's own noble moral feelings without having taken a single step to improve one's own character. . . .

The effects of this perverted form of moralism are potentially diabolical. The new morality makes it quite possible to be a passionate lover of humanity, like a Robespierre, a Marx or a Lenin, and to be a passionate hater of actual human beings. Surely, moral blindness and conceit are wholly dominant when the representative of the heavenly kingdom, the priest who administers the sacraments and preaches the word of love, is considered justified in also carrying a machine gun. "You be my brother or I shall kill you!"

Christians must always remember that earthly progress is not the equivalent of the growth of Christ's Kingdom. Christians must be interested primarily in the eternal designs and transcendent destiny which God plans for man. Central to Christ's Kingdom and the eternal plans of God is personal transformation in Christ. We must bring home to our hearts the truths that Jesus did not die only in the first century, but that he dies today; that the Spirit moved upon the church not only at the beginning, but that he does at the end; that the prime purpose of the God who works in the world at this very hour is the replication of Jesus Christ in the lives of his human creatures; that this world has already been judged and found wanting, and *its willful apostasy taints all its self-improvement schemes.* The Christian's main calling is not to change political systems, to build weapons or to disarm them, to make wealth or to distribute it. The Christian's interest in worldly affairs, as a Christian and not just as an ordinary citizen, must focus on those laws and policies which make it easier or harder for him to fulfill his dual calling—to become a replica of Christ and to witness to others that this is their vocation as well.

As a citizen of this world, the Christian should analyze political programs from the vantage point of the Gospel, and, if they are consonant or at least not dissonant with the Gospel, lend a hand where he can. But one does not paint the house while it is burning down. The secular humanists have marshalled impressive coalitions of dedicated people for painting the house—for improving the externals of human life. Christians have been far less energetic in working to put out the fire—to eradicate spiritual illiteracy and defend God's people against the threats to their well-being and spiritual identity. One is distressed to see so many believers neglecting causes of primary, spiritual importance and expending their energies on causes of secondary, material importance. The moral house of Western civilization is burning down; the spiritual life of millions of people is fading; the public order as a whole is polluted by pandemic indecency. Yet where are the followers of Jesus?

Another danger in embracing the secular agenda exclusively is the possibility *that one might succeed!* The danger in success is that by accomplishing some improvement in man's externals one gets the idea he has thereby improved man himself. Mussolini made the trains run on time, yet he did not thereby bring better government to Italy. The fact is that government is not only a technical enterprise, but is at root a moral enterprise. An evil government can do technically good things, as history abundantly testifies. As a matter of Christian insight, to improve man's externals has nothing directly to do with the essential betterment of man himself, save insofar as the externals—the laws, for example—bear on the spiritual life of the citizenry.

Another danger of too eagerly embracing the secular agenda is the message it gives to non-Christians. When we give them the impression that their agenda and ours are identical, and that improving systems and externals is as important to us as it is to them, we leave them in their spiritual blindness. There is nothing that will challenge the premises of the secularist's life, nothing to remind him that there is a next life, nothing to call his attention to his resistance to the love of the God-Man who died for him. By letting him work against externals solely, we allow him to deepen his blindness to the real nature of the enemy. Our adversaries are not, as our secularist friends believe, the rich, the poor, the system, or "isms." The enemies are, as scripture teaches, beings of great power and malice and intelligence:

> For we are not contending against flesh and blood, but against the principalities, against the powers, against the world rulers of this present darkness, against the spiritual hosts of wickedness in the heavenly places. (Eph 6:12)

It is fashionable nowadays to deny or doubt the existence of a personal devil. Nowhere is this denial more widespread, it seems, than among the intelligentsia who dominate the forming of national opinion and, indirectly, the nation's policy. We Christians do them no favor by pretending that we share their myopia to spiritual reality, or by spending all our energies wrestling against flesh and blood while we let the principalities and powers of wickedness possess the soul of civilization without intense efforts on our part to perform an exorcism. We betray our own calling and our secular humanist friends when we allow them to draft us into the wrong war—the war for a better life on earth at the price of surrender in the war to attain heaven. What does it profit a Christian if he removes air pollution from the whole world, but does nothing about the spiritual pollution of pornography that will cause his and his neighbor's children to lose their immortal souls? What does it profit a Christian if he revives the American economy, only to have Americans spend their extra cash on petty hedonism? What does it profit a Christian if he promotes "peace" in the world, but does nothing about the spiritual war against the principalities and powers and rulers of darkness?

The Dual Calling

The Christian has a dual calling. He must first bring his private life into conformity with the mind of Christ and *also* work to improve the legal, political, financial, and social system of society. In this latter effort, personal piety and private faith are essential, but not sufficient in themselves. Effective action in the world requires practical wisdom, sound political and legal principles, an accurate grasp of the size of a given social problem, and knowledge of past success or failure in solving it.

Many Christians, both Protestant and Catholic, liberal and conservative, have involved themselves energetically in programs for political betterment of mankind without the benefit of such practical wisdom. They justify their position on secular issues with the assumption that their being "right with the Lord" makes their political judgment equally right, no matter how ignorant they are of the workings of the real world they would change. One need not doubt their subjective good faith; the problem is that "good faith" alone is not enough. In general, a godly political order is the result of sustained application of correct natural principles, discernible by Christians both through faith and through their reason, and perceived by reasonable non-Christians as right. For example, assuming that a just social order includes a high measure of material prosperity, Christians must know a good deal about sound economics if they are to influence a just economic policy. Economics is not merely a calculus of the distribution of goods, but is more essentially a way of motivating the initial *production* of goods. The economic naivete of some Christian activists matches their political naivete in the field of "liberation theology," a politicization of the Gospel which tells Christians to make common cause—even violent common cause—with Marxists to overthrow oppressive regimes. This revolutionary enthusiasm ignores the Marxist record: when they come to power, the Marxists have always brought injustice and impoverishment. The political truth is that Marxism does not work. A spiritual truth is that the philosophical/theological inspiration of Marxism is atheist; and one may doubt that the scriptures permit us to yoke ourselves with unbelievers. I have argued earlier in these pages that atheism is not a permissible basis, in God's eyes, for any social order. Any Christian identified with the Lord through prayer and scripture, through liturgy and fellowship, should realize that elemental fact.

The Christian, then, should complement his private faith with a sound public philosophy, founded both on biblical principles and on Christian reason discerning the outlines of the structural necessities in human life. Specifically, both the Bible and sensible social philosophy teach that the family is the essential unit of human endeavor; both the Bible and sound psychology teach that pornography is evil and harmful; both the Bible and sound economics teach that we should not go into inordinate debt and that we must work if we would eat; both the Bible and sensible practical charity suggest that helping the needy is primarily a voluntary and person-to-person task, not primarily a compulsory government-to-citizen task.

It follows that a good Christian citizen must not let his presumed private virtue excuse him from the task of learning political, economic, and legal truth. The Christian airline pilot or engineer must know the principles and dynamics of his field; the Christian physician and the Christian police officer must develop the natural skills to use the ordinary tools the Lord has given them. Civic duty is no different. The Christian citizen must have the wisdom to discern the difference between reformation and deformation of society, between essential and accidental needs, between the collapse of important values and the modification of marginal customs.

Our first civic task as Christians is to preserve the essential spiritual values necessary to provide the context for our own and our children's eternal salvation and to praise God according to the First Commandment. This is a defensive struggle; the secular humanists now occupy the high ground and they have the initiative. We should also be able to contribute to the basic material and economic reformation of society by restoring biblical principles to the financial and governmental policies that provide the material conditions for progress or regress. We have not done well preserving spiritual values in this country; like Paul before his conversion, we have almost stood and held the garments of the executioners. Certainly we have stood largely silent, and only a few Christian writers have dared to speak boldly, as has Franky Schaeffer:

> Christians should be *shamed* by the zealous activity of the liberal elite whose houses are built on sand, while we, with our houses supposedly built on the rock, sit silently and look on. The ACLU aggressively files approximately six thousand . . . often antireligious activist cases a year. . . . Planned Parenthood never rests in their effort to have more abortions performed. . . . All too often the Christian response has been limited to another conference, while the secularist elite is actively engaged in *real events.*[1]

We are similarly ineffective in work for the basic economic reformation of society through biblical principles. It is plain that evangelicals and traditional Catholics have tolerated a chasm between their largely frugal, relatively debt-free private lives and the profligate, indebted public policies they endorse in the voting booth. By and large, we have acted as if there were two sets of economic principles, as if spending more than one's income in the private family would lead to bankruptcy while spending more than one's income in the public government would lead to prosperity. Yet the Bible's general condemnation of excessive indebtedness is universal, and it flies in the face of common sense to believe a government can long spend money it does not have without penalty.[2]

There is a social reformation we must undertake as well. Too long have we tolerated the easy transfer of necessary social tasks such as education and care for the elderly from the family to a remote government. In ordinary cases, these tasks belong in the family. The reason is that they are highly personal and, unlike road building or fire protection, include intellectual and spiritual values the State is incompetent to provide. Now that the secular humanists have largely captured the courts and the government agencies, we have begun to awaken to the fact that we need not have transferred such powers to the highest levels of government in the first place. If we had had the wisdom and the will, we could have legislated policies more in keeping with biblical principles. In education, we could have enacted means of financing family-oriented private schools which could, unlike today's public schools, expressly teach the family's values. In old-age care, we could have enacted tax credits and savings accounts like the recent IRA's, to motivate people to set aside extra funds for their declining years. The Family Protection Act, in the 1981 and 1982 sessions of Congress, contains provisions along these lines.

The principle behind such measures is to move the solution for a problem away from the individual or family, who has responsibility for it, *only* up to the *next* level of social order and *only* when it is necessary. Responsibility should go from the family to the neighborhood or community, then to a city or labor union, then to the state or church, and on up to the national government or national organization. We should always attempt to transfer responsibility back down to "lower" levels of order, and ultimately to the individual or the family once again. Some writers have called this the Principle of Subsidiarity: each "higher" order is subsidiary, because it is helpful to the lower.[3] This principle is entirely consonant with the charity shown by the early Christians as described in Acts and with the moral lessons of both Old and New Testaments. The Christian insists that a person has free will and is to be responsible for himself, and, through charity, is to be responsible to some degree for his neighbor.

In sum, Christians do have something special to offer to public policy. But it is not slavish endorsement of the platform of any one of the political parties. Rather, it is the insistence that policymakers adhere to basic true principles. In order to preach those principles, we must know what they are—and practice them in our own lives.

The Struggle in the Churches

The *first* aspect of the spiritual struggle that confronts us occurs within the Christian church itself. The two contending orientations we have described are visible in the church: Christians who put the Lord and his will and spiritual things first are at serious odds with those Christians who put worldly improvement first. The two camps can collaborate on certain limited projects, and all Christians, as good citizens, should contribute their share of skill and insight to the task of building the City of Man. Nonetheless, the assumptions and purposes of most of that City's architects run counter to the Christian spirit.

This point is well illustrated by the way many denominations and individual Christians have involved themselves in the modern "peace movement." Genuine and just peace is a goal that all well-meaning men and women ardently desire. But peace, for a Christian, is much more than an abstract word summarizing a vague condition of earthly well-being, the freedom to pursue one's private selfishness. Nor can a Christian simply assert that "peace is the work of God" and thus conclude that if we work for "peace" we work for God. The Christian knows that not all peace is from God; the scripture makes it clear that our inclinations to "do good" must be tested by their fidelity to basic Christian perceptions of reality: "Beloved, believe not every spirit, but try the spirits whether they are of God; because many false prophets are gone out into the world" (1 Jn 4:1).

The secular prophets of peace exclude this spiritual dimension from their efforts. They rely almost exclusively on negotiations, treaties, rallies, pressure tactics, letter-writing campaigns, strategic analysis, and the other political tools available in a democratic society. The common spirit linking all these is that they are fundamentally secular, external, *human* steps. They require not the slightest *personal* repentance, conversion, fasting, or prayer. They do not address the spiritual roots of the world's arms problem.

A Christian working for peace must recognize that the cause

of war is not externals; it is sin. The cause of war is not weapons; weapons are the external manifestation of disordered hearts and darkened intellects. The cause of war is man's willful alienation from God and his law.

The Old Testament testifies that war can often be an expression of God's judgment on sinful people. God judged the Hebrews by sending warrior nations such as the Assyrians and Babylonians to afflict them:

> A lion has gone up from his thicket,
>   a destroyer of nations has set out;
>   he has gone forth from his place
> to make your land a waste;
>   your cities will be ruins
>   without inhabitant. (Jer 4:7)

The remedy for this judgment is not an arms buildup or disarmament but a return to God. Immediately after the verse just quoted, Jeremiah tells his people how to avoid the punishment to come:

> For this gird you with sackcloth,
>   lament and wail;
> for the fierce anger of the Lord
>   has not turned back from us. . . .
> O Jerusalem, *wash your heart from wickedness,*
>   *that you may be saved.* (Jer 4:8, 14) [italics added]

The Christian explanation for war is that war is caused by man's sin. Thus the Christian remedy for war is conversion, repentance, prayer, and penance. These are *spiritual*, internal, private, individual, *godly* steps.

The Christian remedy for the ills of the world is more difficult to embrace than the political programs men have devised. It is tempting to believe, as secularists do, that we can have the best of both worlds—public virtue, but private sin. We would like to think, as a bishop recently stated, that we can have peace simply by desiring it badly enough.[4] But the truth is that sinful man cannot obtain love, or wealth, or peace, or anything else of value simply by desiring it. This is what Satan believed, what Adam and Eve believed, and what men in rebellion against God have believed for many millenia. What we desire requires sacrifice, repentance, conversion, and obedience to God.

Our sense of personal sacrifice and obedience to God seems rather shallow in light of the widespread Christian acquiescence in abortion. In 1972 unrestricted abortion was illegal in all fifty states, and although a few such as New York had "liberalized" their law to permit widespread early abortion, no one was really ready for abortion-on-demand to be imposed in 1973 on all those fifty states. Nor could any pro-abortion group have achieved such a change by going to Congress or the state legislatures. With a stroke of a pen, the Supreme Court authorized a slaughter of innocent humans on a scale greater, by 1983, than the infamous Nazi Holocaust in the period 1935-45. It is true that diverse prolife groups have sprung up, populated, it appears, largely (though by no means exclusively) by Christians. Some institutional churches have indeed spoken out against this epic immorality, but the Christian activists working against abortion are a small minority of all Christians. Some Christian denominations have waffled on the issue, protesting, when confronted with the truth about unborn life, like Peter when confronted by the servant girl; they say: "I don't even know him!" (Lk 22:57). The mainline Protestant churches seem especially culpable in this regard.[5] They maintain "social concerns" ministries in many of their congregations, yet they rarely kindle their members to a concern that is unpopular with the press and the national television media, such as a concern for unborn life. But Evangelicals and Roman Catholics cannot escape some criticism. The Evangelicals were late to come to the prolife fight and are still for the most part spectators rather than participants. Catholics have been most active in this struggle, but their bishops have diffused their influence by spreading it randomly into many matters of marginal persuasiveness, and Catholic grassroots organizations in individual parishes often seem to spend more energy in constant tinkering with the liturgy than in purposeful witness to essential moral truths. A striking example of Christian passivity is the astonishing willingness of many Christian churches to accept neopagan sex education instead of resisting it. The churches sometimes try to "baptize" sex education with Christian language, but the result is usually a mixture of sense and nonsense. An example is the recent 118-page booklet, "Education in Human Sexuality for Christians," published by the U.S. Catholic Conference.[6] Among other half-truths, the book offers this philosophical error:

> Knowledge, in itself, is not harmful. Therefore, every major facet of knowledge and values in relation to sexuality should be covered. . . . Consequently, the following goals and objectives include not only such aspects of sexuality as love, intercourse, family planning, responsibility, chastity, Christ, joy, and procreation, but also such subjects as homosexuality, abortion, divorce, rape, prostitution, venereal disease and pornography. (At p. 64)

These "Guidelines" incline toward coeducational classes even in lower grades, and contend apodictically that "in the upper grades, classes should be coeducational" (p. 64). This position ignores the differing levels of maturity between boys and girls at the same age and is largely indifferent to the need to view sex as a private/sacred act. Coed instruction is especially inappropriate for discussion of sexual perversions. This document, which is not the worst of its kind, is nevertheless an archetype, particularly in its bland commentary about "the fundamental goodness of human life as created by God" (p. 67). This point needs—but does not receive—balance by reference to the fact of Original Sin.

This official statement of the institutional office of the nation's largest Christian communion attempts to baptize an essentially anti-Christian program instead of standing against it. But by downplaying or misstating essential Christian truths about sex, this statement does not convert the anti-Christian program of the world; it embraces it and is converted by it![7] This attitude of friendly collaboration instead of courageous resistance characterizes many Christian denominations. By and large, the resistance to neopagan sex education in public schools is not the sustained effort of the churches, but the episodic counterthrusts by outraged individual Christian parents.

Two final examples of Christian acquiescence in neopagan values are noteworthy. The first is the churches' apathy in the face of the pro-homosexual drive to redefine what is normal. In the legal order, Christians have actively supported efforts to obtain actual preference for homosexuals through adding this class of persons to those suffering "discrimination" under the civil rights laws. In the ecclesial order, pressures grow to deny that being an active homosexual disqualifies one from ministry or sacrament. The assumption is that perennial Christian teaching on homosexual practice is repealed by humanist psychology. The second example is the churches' growing willingness to replace the discipline of Christian doctrine with vague feelings of affection as the wellspring of training of the young, whether in grammar school or college. Our children are growing up with the notion that "being a Christian" means "loving" and "loving" means being "outgoing, creative, free, expanding, relational, open." For the modern Christian, as Charlie Brown would say, "Love is a warm puppy."[8] But as Randy Engel remarks,

> While Charlie Brown may be right, there is another type of love which Dostoevski called "a harsh and dreadful thing." . . . the meaning of tough love is the most important thing you'll ever learn and the most important thing you can ever teach children. . . . [Love includes] strength, patience, and personal sacrifice. "Good Friday is a luminous symbol of real love. Wherever there is love, you find a cross, and wherever there is a cross, you find a victim, not a warm puppy." Love and sacrifice are not the same thing, but they are inseparable things. . . . Where love has been preached without sacrifice, it

has led not to love but to license. Where Christ has been preached without the cross, it has led not towards Christ but away from him.[9]

Because in most Christian denominations there is much preaching of love without sacrifice and of Christ without the cross, our churches tolerate license—and our children drift away from Him. No wonder the struggle for the authentic Christian mind in institutional churches, both mainline Protestant and Roman Catholic, is not going well. With notable exceptions, the leaders of the churches are men who seem to find the world's arrangements so broadly unobjectionable and their own congregation's spiritual lives so satisfactory that it need not be said that our earthly home is essentially not safe and comfortable. In times of crisis—and surely we are entering a period of greater crisis than ever before in the world's history—we need bold leaders, men and women afire with the authentic supernatural spirit of Jesus. We Christian layman must struggle to rekindle this supernatural spirit in our own ranks.

The Struggle in Society

The second aspect of the spiritual struggle takes place in the civic arena. This is the conflict between those who would solve society's public problems through unaided human reason alone and those who would solve those problems through the aid of God and the Christian understanding of human nature. Though there can be some overlap, some concurrence, some agreement, by and large these two approaches differ totally. They differ on what the problem is. They differ on the ethical limits of dealing with the problem. They differ on what might be valid answers. And, as we have seen, the secular prescriptions for public well-being are moving inexorably against the Christian presence in civic life.

Consider, for example, how the secular humanists and Christians differ on questions of sexual morality. The secularists say: use more contraceptives, get a divorce, have an abortion. The latter say, control yourself by practicing chastity, be faithful, bear the child. There is no way to bridge these two approaches; they are as different as night and day. They are so different that proponents of each approach regard the other as an enemy.

Consider the secular humanist dealing with pain, suffering, and death. He says, take drugs and tranquillizers, for pain has no value. The secularist is sympathetic to the use of active euthanasia for dying people, on the subject's own terms or perhaps those of a committee. "Man belongs to himself" and has the "right" to decide when he will die. But the Christian sees value in suffering for the sake of Christ. He insists that only God may decide the day and the hour of death, for man belongs to God and only he has the right to determine when an innocent person will die. Again, we see an unbridgeable gap between the Christian and the secularist.

Consider the debate over the future integrity of the family. Nothing in secular humanist ideology would mandate support for the traditional one-man-one-woman-married-under-law family. The secular humanist sees ethics as conventional constructs developed by man through his culture; as mores change so do morals. Consequently the law may support any sexual "familial" arrangement that society wishes to sanction or that insulated and independent courts are willing to recognize. For the Christian, God set up only one valid form of marriage; all others are counterfeit. Once again, we see a chasm that permits no bridge.

If these matters were merely affairs of philosophical specu-lation in Faculty Club easy chairs, there would be a less serious struggle to engage Christians. But ideas have a way of working their way into practice, and practices either violate or comply with law, and law expresses the reflective judgment of the community as to what is "right" and "wrong," permissible and punishable. In other words, the law educates and ideas have consequences. The Christians knows there are set standards and changeless ethical norms; he knows God has condemned some conduct and established other conduct as righteous; he knows that his obedience to God's commands is not optional but rather involves the salvation of himself and others. The world's belief that ethical arrangements change affects behavior and leads to dangerous practical consequences—dangerous to Christians along with everyone else.

The practical consequences of this attitude came home to me a couple years ago in a private discussion with a congressman about the impact of the proposed Equal Rights Amendment on the family as an institution. We disagreed heartily on the merits of the Equal Rights Amendment, but not so strongly on the facts. The congressman acknowledged that E.R.A. would put such issues as public policy about "homosexual marriages" and compulsory draft of women into the military into the hands of unelected federal judges instead of elected legislatures. He further agreed that from their past track record it was fair to predict that these judges would mandate sweeping moral changes. He could foresee such court-ordered measures as legitimization of homosexual marriages (with a corollary right to adopt children) and an order that the U.S. Armed Forces be one-half female. I remarked that these and other public conventions would further wound an already gravely damaged family structure in America. The congressman did not deny it. His answer was: "Then some new social form will arise." It was clear from his tone that he saw no harm in that prospect; he even welcomed it.

In his book *A Christian Manifesto* Francis Schaeffer comments on the new meaning and connotation of pluralism. It now is used to mean that all types of situations are spread out before us, and that it really is up to each individual to grab one or the other on the way past, according to the whim of personal preference. What you take is only a matter of personal choice, with one choice as valid as another. Pluralism has come to mean that everything is acceptable. This new concept of pluralism suddenly is everywhere. There is no right or wrong; it is just a matter of your personal preference. On a recent "Sixty Minutes" program on television, for example, the questions of euthanasia of the old and the growing of marijuana as California's largest paying crop were presented this way. One choice is as valid as another. It is just a matter of personal preference. This new pluralism is presented in many forms, not only in personal ethics, but *in society's ethics and in the choices concerning law.* [10]

The congressman's indifference to the prospect of the collapse of the family order of our society is based on this new pluralism. We should underscore the enormity of this spiritual blindness. Here is a public official—elected in part, one can presume, by Christian voters—who was untroubled by the demise of the family. Through the agency of legislators like this congressman, and judges who share his outlook, the "pluralism" of personal moral preference would become the official policy for a nation that is nominally Christian, a nation in which the majority of the electorate would almost certain assert they *are* Christian. Why do Christians elect pagans to govern them?

In the liturgies of some of the sacramental Christian communions, the celebrant leads the congregation in a public confession of sinfulness. They pray: "I confess to Almighty God, and you, my brothers and sisters, that I have sinned through my own fault, in what I have done, and *in what I have failed to do.*" The confession of sin "for what I have failed to do" reminds us how Christians have abdicated civic responsibility. Though the believing Christian does a fairly conscientious job running his personal affairs and his private family life, it is fair to say that he does not act as responsibly in his life as a citizen of this Republic. In his private life, the believer applies Christian principles; he asks, What does the Lord want me to do here? How would Jesus Christ handle this situation? What do the scripture and the church teach? Answering such questions is not always easy, but at least the Christian realizes he must go to Christianity to find the answers. But Christians do not ask the same questions when judging candidates for office, when voting for local referenda, in writing letters to newspapers, joining political action groups, giving money to candidates, and in the myriad other ways a citizen can affect public policy. By and large, Christians approach such matters with the same outlook as their secularist friends. Christian lawyers come in for special criticism. Francis Schaeffer asks a question which should cause every Christian lawyer to reflect:

> In these shifts that have come in the law, where were the Christian lawyers during the crucial shift from forty years ago to just a few years ago? These shifts have all come, or have mostly come, in the last eighty years, and the great, titanic shifts have come in the last forty years. Within our lifetime the great shifts in law have taken place. Now that this has happened we can say, surely the Christian lawyers should have seen the change taking place and stood on the wall and blown the trumpets loud and clear. A nonlawyer like myself has a right to feel somewhat let down because the Christian lawyers did not blow the trumpets clearly between, let us say, 1940 and 1970.[11]

As a lawyer, I find Dr. Schaeffer's observation correct. Christian lawyers were yawning in their pews while the deChristianization of law was occuring in America. They were matriculating at church-related law schools that were no different in their philosophy from secular law schools. They were congratulating themselves on their personal piety and rectitude while the moral fabric of American society unravelled. Lawyers, like most Christian citizens, were enjoying the spiritual investment of the past, the capital deposited in our national policy and soul by our ancestors, who had indeed created laws that broadly reflected Christian principles—but then our ancestors, like the Deist "Great Clockmaker," having wound up our legal universe, left it to mechanics who neglected to keep it running right. Our country has spent its Christian capital. It is just about bankrupt. Unless Christians quickly deposit an infusion of Christian principles into the law-making and regulatory processes, others will deposit paganism. If Christians do not influence education, non-Christians, ultimately anti-Christians, will. If Christians do not speak out for Christian economic principles, non-Christians will speak out for theirs. The coming struggle is all about the question, Who will set the tone of society, make its rules, declare its "rights" and "wrongs"? Besides the family, other crucial areas where the struggle will take place include education, biological engineering, public morality, and the value or utility of pain, inconvenience, and what might be called "human uselessness." In education, evolution is taught as if it were a fact, not a faith; but creationism receives no "equal time," either as a fact or as a faith.[12] So-called "value-free" sex education goes on in most public school systems, a teaching that is indeed "value-less" and which instructs the children that there is nothing of value associated with sex. In the "values clarification" programs, general normative questions are resolved by a situationist, survival-of-the-fittest, majority-vote ethic.[13] Meanwhile, early dating, rock music,[14] easily available drugs form the cultural context where young people must find their moral path. They face a problem spiritually equivalent to the predicament of the lone explorer groping through a jungle swamp at sundown: he has no map to show the quicksand areas and no native guide with a sharp eye out for poisonous snakes or prowling lions. Realizing the morass from which they must extract their children, many evangelical Protestants and Catholics turn, at great personal sacrifice, to private Christian schools—only to have the state accreditation agencies fight to close them down. Within the public schools themselves, symbolic momentary public prayer is officially impossible, and school administrators frequently prevent voluntary group study of the Bible even in free time.[15] For the majority of citizens, the largest single experience in their child's first twenty years of life—the countless hours he spends in school—contains no systematic encounter with God or scripture even as it contains increasing sympathetic treatment of principles and practices antithetical to the Gospel.

In public morality, in every calendar year abortion kills five times more innocent young Americans than our total combat deaths in World War II. Infanticide, where abortion "fails" or where the child is deformed, now takes place with the tolerance of hospitals and doctors, courts and judges. Fetal experimentation occurs on both deceased (usually aborted) and still alive little human bodies, a kind of scientific cannibalism possible only in a country where the American Medical Association and the American Bar Association have collectively, whatever the rectitude of individual members, denied anything sacred in human life. These various violations of the commandment, "Thou shalt not kill," can occur only because the law has severed its roots in Judeo-Christian theology and history, and because Christian citizens have tolerated that severance or ineffectually opposed it.[16]

Another aspect of public morality is the movement of private vice into public life. No longer are perversions the province of closeted individuals on a small scale. Today hundreds of magazines, video tapes and "home box office movies,"[17] bookstores, theaters, and entertainment centers cater to animal appetites. Yet if Christians were active in public life there would be laws against such things, and where there are laws, they would be enforced. Moreover, if Christians knew how to apply their faith to civic activity, they would not permit the law to abandon its traditional protection of monogamous marriage and adopt, as in practice it has done, toleration of transient "relationships" equivalent to what the law used to call, only a generation ago, "open and notorious adultery."

Finally, in the area of what might be called utility or "human uselessness," the erosion of classic truths has not gone quite as far, but it is on the brink of similar neopagan change. In human affairs we often encounter situations and events and experiences which have no "value" in this world's terms: pain, deformity, retardation, incurable disease, senility, death. The world sees no "use" in such conditions, and the world's patience with the expense entailed in caring for such "useless people"—doctor bills, nursing homes, hospital beds, costly equipment, social security payments, special schools—is wearing thin. At one time the law protected the useless people of our society. Except for unborn children and some retarded or obviously senile adults, the rhetoric of our society still by and large expresses sympathy for them. But we have lost our heart for that game, for it is a game one must believe in. Already in England there are groups promoting "active" euthanasia; their progress is a *déjà vu* of the pro-abortion movement twenty years ago. Like abortion, it seems the stages in their movement would be, first, to make the act socially acceptable, morally tolerable, and legally permissible; then euthanasia would become an act mandatory for social welfare. In America, we have reached the "permissible legally" stage for infanticide of the deformed child. We are at a slightly earlier stage for "active euthanasia."

We Christians ourselves contributed to the neopagan denial of the value of suffering when we handed over to the state so many social welfare functions better handled, in most cases, by the family. We allowed Congress to pass laws which institutionalized charity, taking it out of the hands of the people best situated to perform it and transferring it to strangers. We approved of tax laws that made contributions to hospitals and institutional homes run by strangers tax-deductible, but which gave no tax break to the private family members who took care of their elderly parents in the individual home of one of them but shared the cost among family members so that no one bore over half. We approved the setting up of a Social Security system that compelled every wage earner to give his "security" into the hands of a "Grand Father" or "Big Brother"—the State—rather than simply compelling the person himself, through the tax laws, to set aside his own fund in private insurance/annuity systems and thereby take responsibility for his own future. The Bible puts personal responsibility, private associations and voluntary groups, the family first of all, as the prime providers of social welfare; the secular welfare statist prefers public law, compulsion, and the State as the prime provider of welfare. We Christians voted, by and large, for the secular world's system—and we did it while appealing to the teaching of Jesus Christ! Little wonder then, as we move to an epoch where the world will say that caring for senile old folks and people who are suffering but not "contributing" to society is not "cost-effective," that we have weakened our position: we should have foreseen that to transfer responsibility to the State is to transfer power, and power is always wielded according to moral, or amoral, or immoral values. The coming fight will be fierce. On the one hand will be the secular humanists who want the state to abandon its principled protection of "useless" human life and change the laws to facilitate expeditious "termination" and "disposal" of the "unproductive" who do not manifest a socially approved "quality of life." On the other hand will be the Christians who want the state to renew its principled legal protection of such lives but—if we have some economic wisdom—transfer the financial burden to individuals, families, and private associations. For example, Christians should support laws that not only facilitate adoption of retarded or deformed children but provide economic incentives for adoption. Again, we should work for a "Family Security Act" to supplement and perhaps even supplant Social Security. This would permit adult children to save for their parents' retirement years in privately managed funds, with tax incentives such as proportionate reduction of the child's own social security taxes by the amount set aside for his or her parents. This would transfer the cost of providing security from the state back to the individual, where it belongs. The provider of support would change, but the security would remain the same or increase.[18]

There are Christian answers to the issues of the schools, public morality, abortion, suffering, uselessness in old age, retardation, and death. These answers reflect the inner spiritual values that God has put in his creation. Our body politic will either reflect these values in its laws and policies or its laws and policies will have no soul at all. Earlier I mentioned Dr. Frankenstein's laboratory, depicted fearsomely in the first Frankenstein movie. We may not have realized it when we viewed that film, but the author of the book, Mary Shelley, strove to teach a moral in her story of Frankenstein. Remember the most gripping sequence, the movie script of which is paraphrased below:

The two scientists stand expectantly above a tall man-like figure lying on a laboratory table, his hands manacled at the wrist, his legs similarly bound, electric wires attached to little pegs protruding from his temples. His eyes are closed. He does not breathe. Outside a thunder storm brews. The senior scientist throws a switch; electric current flows; the huge body shudders. He reduces the voltage. Thunder outside. Again he intensifies the shock, up to the generator's danger level. One eye of the creature on the table flutters open. Its hand moves. The scientists are elated. They've done it! They have created human life! On their own, assembled it from cast off parts found in graveyards. Give it more current, quick! don't let him lapse back! The equipment hums, whines, the lights flicker; the hands move; both eyes open; the head turns. The brute strives to sit up. A blank look crosses his face. Then malicious. With a quick exertion he snaps the wrist cuffs, sits up, breaks the anklets; with a swing of one powerful arm he sends the now terrified scientists reeling against their crackling equipment. Sparks fly; flames. The monster stands, knocks them into crashing beakers, tips over equipment. Flames burst out of the wiring. The Frankenstein-thing crashes against the door, his clumsy mindless anger accompanied by the random thunder crashing outside. He forces it open, stumbles up the stairs, bursts out into the forest, whence he will destroy buildings and terrorize the townsfolk.

This horror story is a dramatic metaphor: when man sets out to create himself without reference to God or God's limits, he may build a body but he cannot enspirit a soul. Man's creation has technical skill and power, but lacks reason, ethic, tradition, obedience, fealty, purpose, conscience. The Frankenstein-thing becomes raw power unchained, a parody of the Adam who sprung from the hand of God. He represents every individual who cuts himself off from the transcendent constraints and channels that God has embedded in the nature of things; he represents the monstrous culture and society man will create if Christians do not revive their witness in law and public policy.

* * * * *

The Christian's civil duty in an uncivil society is different from all others. He is called to exorcise the Spirit of the Age.

The Christian's first task is to restore the church to its true mission: witnessing to the reality of the supernatural, bringing man to God, embodying Jesus in the world. The church must stop being preoccupied with the secular side of the secularist agenda. The church's job is to build the Body of Christ, not the City of Man.

The Christian's second task is to restore spiritual and moral truth to public policy. This is the renewal of the spiritual within the secularist agenda; or, better, the modification of that agenda to make it reflect the spiritual.

Restoring the church is possible, with the help of the Holy Spirit, if Christians will use those means that are the Lord's: prayer, worship, Bible study, and spiritual reading. But it will not be easy to convince those in the church, many of them leaders, who have committed themselves to secular solutions to secular problems that there is "one thing necessary" for the church; for they have busied themselves about too many things.

Restoring Christian truth to society will be even harder. Humanly speaking, it is impossible. Any success will be the result of the Spirit overcoming the entrenched resistance to Christian truth that now characterizes the media, the government, the judiciary, and the universities. Unlike the secularized Christians, who at least give lip service to the supernatural, the elite sophisticates in these policy and law-making institutions *resent* Christianity. They resist it. They reject the Christian prescription for man's welfare. They do not want the constraints of God's law to inhibit their "liberty" to do whatever they want with their private lives and to assist in the grand collective project of building the City of Man without God. In this a dual struggle in church and society, the Christian must focus on those laws and policies which make it harder for people to worship God, imitate Christ, and respond to the promptings of the Spirit. It is not the Christian's task to remedy every evil. Spiritual matters are higher than material; the quality of moral life in the populace is more important than the quality of economic life; legal protection for immemorial Christian values and institutions such as the traditional family is more important than the passage of laws which embody some generalized but arguable scheme to produce or redistribute wealth. Followers of Christ must keep asking themselves how their policy preferences are distinctively Christian; they must come to understand that knowing the mind of Christ Jesus is a task of far greater profundity than rote recitation of a few words about loving one's neighbor. In this effort to discern the spirits and adopt the priorities of Jesus, Christians can begin with this negative rule-of-thumb, overstated somewhat: if the policy, program, or law has the enthusiastic and unqualified endorsement and support of the secular humanists, it is probably not what Christians should give their top priority to; as a matter of fact, it often will be something they should oppose. I would argue that there are some organizations in this country that are so well-known for their radical secularism that if a Christian simply opposed their efforts he would be correct 90 percent of the time. This is true of such disparate matters as abortion, aid to education, control of pornography, laws on sexual relationships, the role of religious practice in public schools, so-called "victimless crimes," government involvement in compulsory charity, alternative retirement systems, the entertainment industry, and even promoters of ostensible peace in the world.[19] Still, such an a priori approach is not enough: the educated citizen must have intrinsic reasons for supporting one candidate or policy and opposing another. Nevertheless, the caution that we hesitate to embrace the world's agenda at least reminds us that even those fields where we can make common cause with the secular humanists we might better spend our time and energy on our own distinctive purposes: for if we do not help them in the world's work, there still will be thousands of helping hands; but if *we* do not help promote our own agenda, there will be no one to help us. The humanists surely will not.

Our agenda must include setting up political action groups to promote candidates, legislation, and public attitudes in favor of

—traditional public morality

—protection for unborn children

—a respected place for God in public education —repealing laws and rules that discriminate against private religious education

—a reasonable share of one's own tax money to educate his children according to this conscience and in a schooling environment that reflects his religious values

—the withdrawal of public schools from instruction in areas where their psychological assumptions are dubious, if not false, and the spiritual values they inculcate are amoral, if not immoral (e.g., sex education)

—public policies that give the classical family the preference and encouragement and do not seek to reduce it to just one more "alternate lifestyle" among many which the government treats with equal support

—economic arrangements that encourage individuals and families to solve their own problems and care for their own needs, rather than pass them on to a remote agency of the state

—a national financial policy that reduces public debt and stabilizes our currency so that it maintains real value.

In exorcising the Spirit of the Age from the church and in seeking to keep him at bay in the world, let us not fall into the trap of relying, as he would have us rely, on our own skill, energy, and eloquence. Such reliance would be the ultimate irony: an attempt to wrestle with flesh and blood strength against enemies who are principalities and powers. If we would cast out the Spirit of the Age we must realize "this kind cannot come forth by nothing, but by prayer and fasting" (Mk 9:29).

A Letter to a Christian Citizen

DEAR FELLOW CITIZEN:

The question is, What is the role of the Christian citizen?

The answer in a nutshell is this: the Christian citizen in the United States should be a spiritual and moral leaven in society so that the public order reflects God's own priorities. These priorities are the primacy of spirit over matter, of the next life over this life. Secondarily, God's priorities, I believe, include the mandate to protect the moral order of this world. To a lesser, tertiary extent, the priorities of the Lord also include efforts to better and make more truly human our lives here, remembering all the while the innate limits and incompleteness of all human strivings for paradise on earth.

There are some truths which to the Christian are self-evident: (1) God does exist and he forbids us to build a society based on atheism; (2) the ultimate root of all evil in the world is original and personal sin, and thus redemption (deliverance from evil) will not come from a change of externals or environment but from personal inner conversion; (3) human beings are free and responsible moral agents, and so all collectivist regimes are anti-Christian because they force individuals into a preconceived mold, stress economic determinism, and usually presuppose government-imposed atheism; (4) the "correct" economic plan or legal formula cannot "right" the wrongs of the

193

world because the wellsprings of these evils are the hearts of men; and (5) the individual human person has transcendent value and destiny which the public order of law should respect, and the political order must be limited in its demands for human allegiance and in its absorbtion of human energies.

The public order is man living communally. Put another way, each of us as individuals has his or her "public side"; through tradition, custom, mores, and law we share a community life. This life should honor God even as our private life should honor him. This means this public life should, at a minimum, not draw us away from the Lord, should not make it harder to save our individual souls, should not collectively dishonor God.

Thus the Christian should be concerned about the public order. We should not withdraw and "leave politics to the politicians" because "politics is a dirty business" and "Christians should not allow themselves to become tainted by the world."

The fact is, because we are "in" the world, though, one hopes, not "of" it, the world already has plenty of chances to taint us. Like an army sitting still, we become an easy target. If we do nothing about the economic, political, and legal rules that structure our public life and much of our private lives, we abandon those rules by default to the manipulation of people who have a theological agenda and a social vision hostile to our faith. We can no more stand aloof, above the fray, when "good" or "bad" laws are made than we could walk by on the other side of the road when we come upon a traveler beaten, robbed, and left half-dead in the ditch. We are called to intervene.

However, we are not called to do all possible "good." There are priorities. There is a hierarchy of "goods" that might be pursued and, in some cases, actually achieved. Random or effusive endeavors to "do good" may well violate the principle of stewardship of our time and talents. Metaphorically: we must be rifles, not shotguns. Just as we are to put our own lives in order—body subject to soul, and both subject to spirit, and the whole subject to the Lord—so also we must put our political and legal priorities in order. We need not do all possible good, but we should do all the *Christian good* possible. Some goods are not distinctively Christian.

For example, like yourselves, I receive in the mail countless appeals for "good causes"—cancer research, blind people, starving children in Africa, groups seeking to preserve and clean up the physical environment, and so forth. Though all of these are "good causes," and it hurts one's heart not to be able to support them all financially, their common denominator is the desire to improve the material well-being of life in this world. This is truly a good. But it is not the highest good a person could support.

There is another set of appeals that I receive through the mail. These include requests for funds for a priest in New York running a halfway house for runaway children trying to escape the clutches of the pornography and prostitution rackets, for missionaries in India, ministers sending Bibles into Russia, campus ministries for Christ, and prison ministries. These also are truly good causes. In my judgment, they are of a higher order than the former, for the common denominator is the desire to bring souls to Christ.

It seems to me that if you must make a choice because you have limited funds, as Christians you should support as many of these appeals as possible and regretfully discard the appeals that lack a spiritual purpose. "What does it profit a man if he gain [or improve] the whole world, yet suffer the loss of his [or others] immortal soul?"

The same principle of proper priorities applies to political candidates. Every other year the nation begins its extended agony of choosing its legislators, and the campaign for president begins about two years before the election. In most cases, the candidates are neither knaves nor fools; members of both political parties running for office are good people who sincerely desire to do good once elected. How should we choose among them?

For many years not a few Evangelicals stayed out of politics. Politics is dirty, many said, and the result doesn't matter much anyhow. Many ethnic Roman Catholics and southern Baptists automatically voted for one political party because it was the party their father and grandfather voted for; many northern Protestants tended, for the same reason, to vote for another party. Other Christians gravitated toward those candidates who promised the most material improvement of life: "a chicken in every pot," "full employment," "lower interest rates," "peace and prosperity," and so on.

It should be obvious that such cultural inertia is an unworthy basis for a Christian, indeed for any citizen, to sign away his vote. Parties and policies and candidates change; though labels may remain the same, the real issues are their impact on the moral environment and their basic grasp of sound economic principles (which happen to be consonant with biblical teaching).

Perhaps less obvious, but equally true, is the fact that a Christian should not sign away his vote to a candidate simply because he promises the most material improvement of life. The Christian should have a broader perspective for political decisions than personal self-interest. If the political appeal amounts to a claim that voters can get something for nothing, the Christian should be suspicious of it as a flawed grasp of economic reality. The art of self-governance should be more than just the rearrangement of material goods so that, somehow, we are all more comfortable and therefore can pursue our petty private hedonisms with more purchasing power. Furthermore, a flawed economic theory, like an arrow mis-aimed at the bow, will not achieve its purpose and may well do considerable harm downrange.

Without taking political sides in a current controversy, I would simply observe that Christians should be alarmed at the principles underlying a system which has seen the government spend more money than it takes in for most of the last fifty years. Scripture and the teaching of the Christian churches tell us to live within our means and to be good stewards of the world's goods. Is it a coincidence that the abandonment of these principles in national fiscal policy has coincided with the demise of the Puritan ethic and the rise of secular humanism as the guiding national philosophy? I think not. I think it is time for Christians to use their votes against candidates whose appeal is based primarily on greed. We should use our influence to change the spectacle of a government at the mercy of contending interest groups, who resemble pigs shouldering each other out around a feeding trough.

These economic questions deal with management of material resources—the body. What of the "soul" of our nation? The nation is not just a grand machine; politics is not merely the science of tuning all the components so that the machine runs smoothly. This is the technocratic notion of politics which dominates the thinking of certain leaders in both parties. Rather, politics is a moral enterprise; it affects the spiritual life distinguishable from the materially comfortable life. The scripture teaches plainly: "Not by bread alone does man live, but by every word that proceeds out of the mouth of God" (Mt 4:4). During the 1930s, the nation endured the greatest collapse of material living standards in its history; during the 1960s and 1970s, the nation enjoyed a time of its greatest material abundance. Yet I ask you, as a Christian, during which period of time was the nation more moral, more pleasing to God? Look at the today's incidence of crime, drug use, pornography, abortion, broken marriages, delinquency. The answer is incontestable.

It seems to me that Christians should evaluate appeals for votes in the same way that I suggest we evaluate appeals for donations: set aside all those promises of a better material life and look for candidates who address the spiritual and moral crisis of our country. The material issues are important, but we should worry more about the soul than about the body.

It seems to me that the great flaw of the first two years of the Reagan administration was to compress its agenda and mandate into the one-dimensional material world of economic policy. Though elected in part by the votes of traditional Catholics and disaffected Evangelicals concerned about the moral breakdown of our country, the Republicans put all their eggs in the economic basket. Doing this was a strategic mistake, I believe, because it reduced their moral leadership to an accountant's balance-sheet, and it put the ultimate control of their destiny in the hands of international bankers, Japanese auto-makers, Arab oil sheiks, the "out-of-control" entitlements programs, and other forces not responsive to managerial persuasion. The Republican technocrats around the president, apparently with his acquiescence, abandoned the moral reform that characterized the party's own 1980 platform. Their success in economic matters has been at best mixed. More importantly, their approach signalled a continuation of the managerial as opposed to moral-leadership style of government—the triumph of pragmatics over principle.

I suggest that we Christians should primarily concern ourselves, in domestic matters, about spiritual and moral questions: crime, law enforcement against drug use and pornography, social initiatives to heal broken marriages, the lack of public prayer and ethical teaching in our public schools, governmental hostility to religious private schools, the tragedy of permissive abortion killing over a million helpless human beings annually.

The Christian's concern should stem, minimally, from notions of self-defense. Remember, the army that stands still is an easy target. The problems just enumerated impinge on the Christian parent; if we would raise children who love the Lord, we must confront the paganism that is the common theme of all these problems. If we fritter away our votes and our energies on candidates who can do no more than promise us economic improvement, we join ranks with the good humanists to whom economic betterment is the *summum bonum*. Let us not sell our birthright for a few pieces of silver—or, these days, a few pieces of paper money. As the moral evils that so corrupt our country become widespread in our own neighborhoods—drug-use and pornography, for example—we would band together (I hope!) with our neighbors to reverse the slide into decadence. We should do no less even though the corruption may be geographically farther away.

Furthermore, the secular state is no longer "neutral" to Christianity. This point is hard to get across to many Christians;

like the frog placed in lukewarm water that was gradually heated to boiling, we do not see how radically our country has changed. The government has now made itself, spiritually, our enemy. If anything should be clear to the readers of this book, it is that whole segments of our governing apparatus—the federal judiciary, the educational administrators, the media elite, and much of the governmental bureaucracies in charge of tax-collecting and educational regulation—are by and large hostile to Judeo-Christian principles and values. Moreover, many Christians in these and other branches of society's leadership elites—such as lawyers who make rules and doctors who deal with ultimate ethical questions—have absorbed the materialism of their peers to such an extent that they allow the world to set the agenda for the church. In short, many Christians think that the Christian's calling is to do no more than imitate the faddist enthusiasms of their secularized fellow citizens. As someone has quipped, too many Christians pride themselves on being "trendier than thou"; they are indeed "salt which has lost its savor." Such Christians are all the more dangerous to the true Gospel because they seem to live "good" lives—of works, not faith—and because they retain enough of the Christian residue to enable them to invoke a blessing here or quote a scripture text there on behalf of the secular platform of this-world improvements. But these "improvements" are almost invariably at the cost of doing nothing for, and often doing harm to, the spiritual quality of our lives. Where are the Christian doctors who should have resigned *en masse* from the American Medical Association when it endorsed abortion on demand? Where are the Christian lawyers who should have protested loud and long when spokesmen for the Individual Rights Committee of the American Bar Association endorsed what boiled down to legal emancipation for all children? Where are the Christian congressmen and senators who should have supported the Family Protection Act, so that some of the power of government can be put to the service of monogamous marriage instead of to its harm? Where for that matter was the "born-again" Christian president in the late 1970s when the I.R.S., over which he had control, launched its attack on Christian schools?

Assuming, as I do, that most of these persons are *privately* "good Christians," I can only conclude that they are philosophical schizophrenics. They have two minds: their private and family mind for home and Sunday mornings; their public and social mind for work and public affairs. This is the only way I can explain the priest and those other Christian congressmen, senators, and judges, who say, for example, that they are "privately opposed" to abortion but publicly support it. The doleful fact is that Christians in government, medicine, law, and the media do not know how to translate their private principles into public acts. It is also clear that many Christians do not really hold their private principles very deeply.

What principles, then, should govern Christians' efforts to confront this clear and present danger? One lesson is that we should stop supporting transfers of responsibility from the individual and the family to the state. Every transfer of responsibility is a transfer of power. No one wields power in a vacuum; he uses it to further his values. If we vote for people and policies who promise to use the compulsory power of the state to educate our children for us or to care for us in our old age, and transfer power to the state, let us realize that there is a price to pay for these supposed benefits. The price is control over the framework of values and the philosophical conditions in which benefits are doled out. The price, for instance, of public schools run by the government is that government excludes the Ten Commandments and includes "value-free" sex education. The price of transferring most health-care from private hospitals and medical schools to those run by government is that government will try to run these facilities according to a "quality of life" ethic. It will exclude medical people who oppose abortion, because government has adopted encouragement of abortion as national policy. The price also has to be paid for even desirable governmental actions, such as national enforcement of civil rights laws. We have seen the power government has gained in this area now used to make Christian schools and churches stop "discriminating" against persons whose sexual conduct is absolutely condemned by the Bible. The price for letting the federal government get involved in family policy is the White House Conference on the family a few years back, which defined the family as "any group of two or more people who care for one another and live under the same roof," a pagan statement which made the family no more than a dormitory club, with no commitment to the traditional concept of one man legally married to one woman.

Christians must learn that we cannot continue to give government responsibility for and consequent power over any area of life with a significant value component without yielding to the government control of the values that go with the program, policy, or law. The government will invariably, over the long haul, impose pagan values.

The Christian Agenda for the next decade must include starting to pull the state out of all social/economic areas where it imposes values. True liberals, who espouse liberty and pluralism, should welcome the effort, for it should be obvious that the state uses compulsion and promotes monopoly. (It has been decades, for instance, since "*all* points of view" on spiritual or moral matters were actually taught in America's public schools.)

The Christian Agenda should include the corollary: limit the state to those public areas of agreement where values are at a bare minimum and where only the state (i.e., government) can do an adequate job; this policy would limit government to such fields as road-building, police protection, internal judiciary, the currency, and, of course, national defense. The state should get out of the fields of monopolizing or moving toward monopoly over the provision of education, health care, housing, old age security, curriculum development, abortion funding.

In the same vein, Christians should promote the decentralization and private provision of social services and education. This does not mean the government "does nothing"; it does mean that the government should provide incentives and encouragement to individuals, families, and private associations to handle these matters and freedom to set the moral tone of social services and education. For instance, tax credits for private school tuition would be a government action, but it would leave the control and educational decision-making in the hands of private individuals and groups. Again, government could ease the burdens of working mothers by offering employers business-expense deductions for employer-provided day-care centers at the place of work. This would allow working mothers to visit their children during lunch and coffee breaks and generally oversee the supervision of their offspring. Another example: through changes in the Tax Code we could encourage workers to save for the old age retirement and health needs of their parents, thus fostering personal responsibility and decentralized planning for social ends. (The Individual Retirement Account, IRA, allows a citizen to exclude $2,000, or, in some cases, $2,250, from taxation each year, if deposited in his *own* IRA. The next step should be to motivate a person to save for his parents' retirement.)

We Christians often neglect another dimension to good citizenship: affecting the direction of public events on a day-to-day basis, not just at election time. Restoring Christian values to our political order, like maintaining personal health, must go on *daily* and follow *specific* steps. Here is a checklist of things you and other members of your congregation could be doing:

—run for local school board

—set up Christian schools

—donate professional time for Christian causes (lawyers, help set up those schools; realtors, help find the sites; doctors, counsel the truth about abortion)

—organize a letter-writing committee to petition representatives on matters of interest to Christians. Write personalized and respectful letters on one topic at a time to local, state, and federal elected officials. Then follow through with a phone call.

—organize a Christian legal committee to take legal steps to preserve your right to control your children's education or to represent you at public hearings. There is nothing wrong with pursuing your rights in court or commission; the ACLU does it constantly for its theological viewpoint.

—establish a Private Charity Trust in each local church, to handle donations for specific needy families and to provide (along with traditional charity) free legal aid for the poor. See James 1:27.

—join and financially support at least one national organization that educates congressmen and the public to Christian positions on such moral matters as abortion, pornography, school prayer, hedonism on television, the public benefits of private schools, and protecting the family.

Organizations which address these issues perform an essential service: they keep the struggle alive after the election by focusing the disparate energies of individual believers through a national headquarters and onto specific officerholders. Some engage in legal defense of Christian values when attacked in the courts; they keep interest high between elections; they develop mailing lists of supporters; their monthly publications keep morale up; they give part-time supporters, which perforce must be most of us, a way to aggregate our small efforts into a large impact.

Remember, we are called to be good citizens. Unlike the period of the Roman Empire, good citizens in our era are expected to become involved in public questions. Indeed, as the civil rights movement has reminded us, good citizens are expected to assert their rights. In a democratic republic, the citizens are, at root, the governors. Along with our non-Christian friends, we Christians have been anointed with the power to rule; we have been given stewardship over our country. If we fail to exercise this responsibility we will be like the steward who took the talent the Master gave him and, instead of investing it for a return, buried it in the ground. This use of the powers God has placed upon us must, however, be done with and in the Lord; for he has said, "I am the vine, and you are the branches; without Me you can do nothing." Thus we cannot exercise proper civic stewardship without keeping our union with the Lord through prayer, scripture study, liturgy, and Christian fellowship.

In conclusion, let me challenge you. We must have the discernment to realize and face up to what is going on in the age we live in. Jesus said: "Ye can discern the face of the sky; but can ye not discern the signs of the times?" (Mt 16:3). We must also have the courage to stop merely talking about the problem and instead stand up and take a firm position in action:

> Decide today whom you will serve, the [pagan] gods your ancestors worshiped in Mesopotamia or the [pagan] gods of the Amorites, in whose land you are now living. *As for my family and me, we will serve the Lord.* (Jos 24:15)

Emphasis is added by each of us.

SINCERELY,

YOUR BROTHER IN THE LORD

Notes

Chapter Two
Christians and the Political World

1. Francis Schaeffer, *How Should We Then Live?* (Revell, 1976), p. 40.
2. At one time a Federal District Judge in New York ruled that the U.S. Congress *must* appropriate tax money to pay for abortions. The Supreme Court, by a 5-4 vote, reversed the ruling, but the principle remains: the secular state claims the right to force Christians, if it wishes, to pay for conduct they believe is manifestly immoral.
3. William Richards, "Free Speech and Obscenity Law: Toward a Moral Theory of the First Amendment," 123. *University of Pennsylvania Law Review* 46 (1974).

Chapter Four
The Courts and God

1. 5 U.S. (1 Cranch). 137 (1803).
2. This is a recurring theme among commentators of all persuasions. See, e.g., Philip B. Kurland, "Government by Judiciary," *Modern Age,* Fall 1976, p. 358; Louis Lusky, *By What Right?* (1975); Gino Graglia, *Disaster by Decree* (1976); Nathan Glazer, "Towards an Imperial Judiciary," *The Public Interest,* Fall 1975, p. 104; Raoul Berger, *Government by Judiciary* (1975).
3. George W. Carby, "The Supreme Court, Judicial Review, and Federalist 78," *Modern Age,* Fall 1974, p. 356.
4. Letter to Abigail Adams, Sept. 11, 1804, in Paul L. Ford, ed., *The Writings of Thomas Jefferson,* 10 vols., 8:310.
5. Letter to William C. Jarvis, Sept. 28, 1820; Ibid., 10:160.
6. The Federalist Papers, #78.
7. *Roe v. Wade,* 410 U.S. 113 (1973), inventing the "right" of abortion-on-demand; *Engel v. Vitale,* 370 U.S. 421 (1962), and *Abington School Dist. v. Schempp,* 374 U.S. 203 (1963), making public school prayer and Bible reading "unconstitutional"; *McCollum v. Board of Education,* 333 U.S. 203 (1948), striking down "released time" teaching of religion on public school premises, though voluntary; most anti-pornography cases, including even

Miller v. California, 413 U.S. 15 (1973), widely seen as pro-morality, but limiting community control of pornography to the "hard core."

8. See the incisive analyses of the philosophy of Hollywood's most influential TV writers, producers, and executives, in Michael Robinson, "Prime-Time Chic," *Public Opinion,* Mar/May 1979, pp. 42-47; L.S. Lichter, S. Robert Lichter, and Stanley Rothman, "Hollywood and America: The Odd Couple," *Public Opinion,* Dec./Jan. 1983, and Ben Stein, *The View from Sunset Boulevard* (New York: Basic Books, 1975).

9. See the author's "Governing the Judiciary," in P. McGuigan and R. Rader, eds., *A Blueprint for Judicial Reform* (Free Congress and Research Foundation, 1981), p. 37.

10. This was International School of Law, which some Evangelical laymen started. Accreditation pressures forced them to give it to the state of Virginia and abandon their efforts. It is now George Mason University Law School and has no distinctive philosophy.

11. See Edward S. Corwin's classic essay, "The 'Higher Law' Background of American Constitutional Law," 42 *Harvard Law Review* 149 (1928).

12. Ibid.

13. James Madison, "A Bill of Rights Proposed" (June 8, 1789), reprinted in 3 *The Annals of America* 354 (Encyclopedia Britannica, 1968), at 358. This view is compelled by the context here, and by the historical fact that "substantive" due process did not arise until roughly one hundred years *after* the Bill of Rights was adopted.

14. 198 U.S. 45 (1905).

15. 268 U.S. 510 (1928).

16. 381 U.S. 479 (1965).

17. Learned Hand, *The Bill of Rights* (1958), p. 70, cited by Justice Black in his dissent in *Griswold.* He also observed: "One of the most effective ways of diluting or expanding a constitutionally guaranteed right is to substitute for the crucial word or words of a constitutional guarantee another word or words more or less flexible." This was the Court's technique in inventing a generalized "right of privacy." See also Hyman Gross, "The Concept of Privacy," *N.Y. University Law Review* 42 (1967), p. 42.

18. 405 U.S. 438 (1972).

19. 394 U.S. 557 (1969).

20. 410 U.S. 113 (1973).

21. See the articles by modern fetologists in T.W. Hilgers, M.D., D.J. Horan, D. Mall, *New Perspectives on Human Abortion* (Frederick, Maryland: University Publications of America, 1981).

22. See the illuminating discussion of the contrast between Planned Parenthood's early and recent views on the evil of abortion in John T. Noonan, *A Private Choice: Abortion in America in the Seventies* (The Free Press, 1979), pp. 36-38.

23. "A New Ethic for Medicine and Society," *California Medicine*, Sept. 1970, pp. 67-68.
24. *Doe v. Bolton*, 410 U.S. 179 (1973).
25. For an incisive critique of the new secular theology animating the modern state, see the writings of R.J. Rushdoony. Particularly worth meditation is his proposition that "the structure of a state represents, implicitly or explicitly, a particular religion." Quoted in John W. Whitehead, *The Second American Revolution* (David C. Cook, 1982), p. 103.

Chapter Five
Church and State: The Struggle for the Schools

1. William Cohen and John Kaplan, *Constitutional Law*, 2nd ed. (Foundation Press, 1982), p. 402.
2. See, e.g., Mark DeWolfe Howe, in *Religion and the Free Society: The Constitutional Question* (Center for Democratic Institutions/Fund for the Republic, 1960). Also, Howe, *The Garden and the Wilderness: Religion and Government in American Constitutional History* (University of Chicago Press, 1965).
3. The argument that the states should be equally bound by both clauses is ably set forth by the nation's leading "separationist," Leo Pfeffer, in *Church, State and Freedom* (Beacon Press, 1953).
4. Jefferson said to Rev. Samuel Miller, XI, *The Writings of Thomas Jefferson* (Andrew Lipscomb Co., 1903-04, issued under the auspices of the Thomas Jefferson Memorial Association), p. 428, italics added.
5. James McClellan, "The Making and Unmaking of the Establishment Clause," in McGuigan & Rader, eds., *A Blueprint for Judicial Reform* (Free Congress Research & Education Foundation, Washington, D.C., 1981), p. 295, 324. This article is an excellent summary of the Founders' attitude, which was to encourage religion to play a major role in society, but "officially" only on the state level.
6. This is the position of Justice Rutledge, dissenting in *Everson v. Board of Education*, 330 U.S. 1 (1947), and of a continuing plurality, frequently majority, of today's Court.
7. See Neal Devins, "A Fundamentalist Right to Education?" *The National Law Journal* (Feb. 21, 1983), p. 13.
8. See the dissent by Justice Reed in *McCollum v. Board of Education*, 333 U.S. 203 (1948), and Justice Stewart in *Engel v. Vitale*, 370 U.S. 421 (1962).
9. 330 U.S. 1 (1947), 15-16, italics added.
10. 333 U.S. 203 (1948).
11. For a comparable view, see Whitehead and J. Conlan, "The Establishment of the Religion of Secular Humanism and Its First Amendment Implica-

tions," *Texas Tech Law Review* 10 (1978), p. 18.

12. The historical summary is dependent in part upon the superb monograph by Dr. Daniel D. McGarry, *Secularism in American Public Education and the Unconstitutionality of Its Exclusive Governmental Support*, available from Social Justice Review, 3835 Westminster Pl., St. Louis, Mo. 63108.

13. See also, John Dewey, *A Common Faith* (Yale University Press, 1934); Corliss Lamont, *The Philosophy of Humanism* (Frederick Ungar, 1972).

14. 367 U.S. 488 (1961).

15. 380 U.S. 163 (1965).

16. There took place in 1983 a case in New Jersey in which the American Civil Liberties Union attacked a "moment of silence" in class at the beginning of the school day because during that snippet of time some children might *think* a prayer!

17. To understand the aggressive strategy of those who have largely driven religion out of our schools, the Christian should read the brilliant analysis by Frank J. Sorauf, *The Wall of Separation: The Constitutional Politics of Church and State* (Princeton University Press, 1976). This book is available from the Christian Legal Society, P.O. Box 2069, Oak Park, Ill. 60603.

18. In New Jersey, in *Tudor v. Board of Education*, 100 A.2d 857 (1953); the same action was attacked in the Florida case, *Brown v. Orange County Board of Education*, 128 So. 2d 181 (1960), 155 So. 2d 371 (1963).

19. As long ago as 1967 a public school teacher in a Chicago suburb informed me that an attorney had immediately called her after she had read Luke's gospel nativity narration, without comment, to the school children a few days prior to the Christmas vacation. He insisted that she cease and desist because allegedly she had violated the Constitution.

20. *Lemon v. Kurtzman*, 403 U.S. 612 (1971).

21. *Meek v. Pittenger*, 421 U.S. 349 (1975).

22. 413 U.S. 76 (1973).

23. One scholar, Edward M. Gaffney, Jr., has termed this, in an article so titled, "Fear of Imaginable but Totally Implausible Evils"; see Kommers and Wahoske, *Freedom and Education: Pierce v. Society of Sisters Reconsidered* (University of Notre Dame Law School, 1978), p. 79.

24. *Wolman v. Walter*, 433 U.S. 229 (1977).

25. 268 U.S. 510 (1925).

26. *Wisconsin v. Yoder*, 406 U.S. 205 (1972).

27. See the publications of Citizens for Educational Freedom, Washington Building, Washington, D.C.; and of the Education Voucher Institute, 2500 Packard, Ann Arbor, Mich. 48104. Both promote the tax credit and the "voucher," which is like a scholarship to be used at the school of one's choice. Other sources of information include the Center for Independent Education, P.O. Box 2256, Wichita, Kans. 67201; the Council for Educational Freedom in America, 2105 Wintergreen Ave., S.E., Washington, D.C. 20028.

See also, John E. Coons and Stephen D. Sugarman, *Education by Choice: The Case for Family Control* (Berkeley: University of California Press, 1978); E.G. West, *Non Public School Aid* (Lexington, Mass.: D.C. Heath & Co., 1976); Dr. Onalee McGraw, *Family Choice in Education: The New Imperative,* available from the Heritage Foundation, 214 Massachusetts Ave., N.E., Washington, D.C. 20002; and *Educational Freedom* (Spring-/Summer 1981), available from the Educational Freedom Foundation, 20 Parkland, Glendale, Mo. 63122.

28. *Federal Register,* 43 163 (August 22, 1978), 37296-7-8. See also the proposed S.995 "Private School Non-Discrimination and Due Process Act" of 1979, *Congressional Record* 125, no. 48 (April 24, 1979), introduced by Senators Schweiker, Helms, et al., on April 24, 1979; and the "Save Our Schools Act," *Congressional Record* 125, no. 23 (Jan. 18, 1979), introduced by Senator Hatch et al.

29. That funds denial, which took the form of an amendment to an appropriations bill, was not added in 1982.

30. E.g., *State of Vermont v. LaBarge,* 134 VT-276 (1976); *Rudasill v. Kentucky State Board of Education,* 589 S.W. 877 (1979); *North Carolina v. Columbus Christian Academy,* No. 78 CVS-1678 (N.C. Super. Ct. Sept. 5, 1978), vacated No. 114, Spring term 1979 (N.C. Super. Ct., May 4, 1979). At this writing, a Baptist pastor in Nebraska is in and out of jail repeatedly because he runs a small Christian school that is not "accredited."

31. To understand the essentially defensive position we are in, see Charles E. Rice, "Conscientious Objection to Public Education: The Grievance and the Remedies," *B.Y.U. Law Review* 847 (1978).

32. See Lynn Buzzard and Samuel Ericsson, *The Battle for Religious Liberty* (Elgin, Ill.: David C. Cook, 1982).

33. Whitehead, *The Second American Revolution* (1982), p. 173. This book is must reading for any Christian who wants to understand how courts are dechristianizing America.

Chapter Six
Christianity and the Sexual Revolution

1. Donald Demarco, in *Fidelity* (February 1982), p. 11.

2. William Stanmeyer, "Obscene Evils v. Obscure Truths: Some Notes on First Principles," 7 *Capital University Law Review* 647 (1978).

3. *M.D. Magazine,* June 1978, p. 11. Dr. Wertham has been an Associate in Psychiatry, Johns Hopkins Medical School; and consulting psychiatrist at Queens Hospital Center in New York.

4. See *Miller v. California,* 413 U.S. 15 (1973).

5. Organizations through which Christians can act include Citizens for Decency through Law, 2331 W. Royal Palm Rd., Phoenix, Ariz. 85021; Morality in Media, 475 Riverside Dr., N.Y.; and National Federation for

Decency, P.O. Box 1398, Tupelo, Miss. 38801. CDL provides skilled attorneys to assist local prosecutors and has an impressive record of success in using laws to discourage pornography.

6. *Hobolth v. Greenway,* 52 Mich. App. 682, 218 N.W. 2d 98 (1974).
7. See the discussion of the Christian parent's dilemma in sending his child to a compulsorily non-Christian school, in: Charles E. Rice, "Conscientious Objection to Public Education: The Grievance and the Remedies," *Brigham Young University Law Review* 847 (1978).
8. See Eugene F. Diamond, M.D., "Teaching Sex to Children," *Columbia Magazine,* June 1981, p. 34. Doctor Diamond makes these points:

   I was involved for 15 years in a program of sex education for engaged couples, for ten years as an instructor in a high-school marriage course and for five years as conductor of a course for eighth-grade children for my own local school board.
   All this activity has convinced me that group sex education is not only useless but counterproductive. . . .
   There is almost a total lack of scientific evidence or statistical data to justify the inclusion of sex education in a school curriculum. Most children in the world will learn about sex from a peer group or a slightly older child. Yet there is no evidence . . . that those educated by these so-called vulgar sources have more sexually transmitted diseases, more illegitimacy, more divorces, more perversions or more sexual failures than those who receive their training in the . . . public-school classroom.

9. The goal of changing moral attitudes is admitted by the proponents of sex education. See, e.g., D. Kirby, J. Alter, and P. Scales, "An Analysis of U.S. Sex Education Programs . . ." Report No. CDC-2021-79-DK-FR, prepared under Contract No. 200-78-0804 by Mathtech, Inc., 4630 Montgomery Ave., Bethesda, Md. 20014, for the U.S. Department of Health, Education, and Welfare, Public Health Service, Center for Disease Control, Atlanta, Ga. 36333 (July 1979).
10. See Claire Chambers, *The Siecus Circle,* Western Islands Pub., Belmont, Mass. 02178 (1977), available from: Sun Life, Thaxton, Va. 24174; this is an analysis of the philosophy and organizations involved in promoting sex education.
11. Judith B. Echaniz, et al., *"When Schools Teach Sex": A Handbook for Evaluating Your School's Sex Education Program* (Free Congress Research and Education Foundation, 1982), available also from Family-Life Culture and Education Council, P.O. Box 8466, Rochester, N. Y. 14618.
12. Rhoda L. Lorand, Ph.D., "A Psychoanalytic View of the Sex Education Controversy," *Journal of the New York State School Nurse Teachers Association,* vol. 2 (Fall 1970), 13, 24. Available from NYSSNTA, 23 Point View Dr., East Greenbush, N. Y. 12061.

13. Melvin Anchell, M.D., "So What's Wrong With the Cave Man?" privately published booklet (1971), p. 7. Dr. Anchell is the author of *Sex and Sanity* (Macmillan, 1971).

14. Christians should consult K.D. Whitehead, *Agenda for the "Sexual Revolution"* (available from Franciscan Herald Press, 1434 W. 51st St., Chicago, Ill. 60609); Suzanne B. and Richard D. Glasgow, "An Expose of Planned Parenthood's Three-Lane Road to the Brave New World," A Special Report, The Human Life Education Fund, Inc., P.O. Box 1565, Altoona, Pa. 16603; and Lorene Collins, "New Light on an Old Problem," *Our Family Magazine*, May 1980, p. 2, who demonstrates that "for anyone who has a Christian view of the human personality, classroom sex education is not merely improper; it is impossible." This article is available from C.U.F., P.O. Box 6361, Edmonton, Alberta T5B 4K7, Canada.

15. On the related matter of proper sex roles, see Harold M. Voth, M.D., "Women's Liberation, Cause and Consequence of Social Sickness," *New Oxford Review*, December 1980, p. 8. The refusal in sex education classes to be "judgmental" about homosexual and lesbian practice, and the covert (and overt) promotion of childlessness while encouraging girls to be as "sexually active" as young men all combine to promote a unisex outlook. Dr. Voth states: "The current trend toward unisexualism and even outright role reversal reflects psychological disturbance on a grand scale." Dr. Voth is Senior Psychiatrist and Psychoanalyst at the Menninger Foundation, Clinical Professor of Psychiatry at the University of Kansas, and author of *The Castrated Family*.

16. See Jacqueline Kasun, "Turning Children into Sex Experts," *The Public Interest*, Spring 1979; also, Ernest van den Haag, "Birds, Bees, and Bathroom Tours," *National Review*, December 7, 1979, p. 1555-57, quoting the Kasun article:

> "The curriculum guide [drawn up for schools in Ferndale, California] suggests that high-school students work as boy-girl pairs on 'physiology definition sheets' in which they define 'foreplay,' 'erection,' 'ejaculation,' and similar terms. Whether or not students are satisfied with the 'size of [their] sex organs' is suggested as a topic of class discussion in this curriculum."
>
> [Dr. van den Haag continues:] These discussions are to help seventh-graders to make an "Intelligent Choice of a Sexual Life Style" by selecting a "personal standard of sexual behavior," apparently from a menu offered by their sex teacher. Religious or moral rules other than self-expression and "live and let live" are not part of what is offered. Self-gratification (expression) is the approved norm. I cannot imagine a worse way to prepare young people for adult relationships, marriage, or family living.
>
> Homosexuality is approved and, like masturbation, is prominent

among the selections offered. In "Sex in Adolescence: Its Meaning and Its Future," distributed to high-school teachers by Planned Parenthood, author James W. Maddock stresses that "we must finish the contemporary sex "revolution" . . . our society must strive to sanction and support various forms of intimacy between members of the same sex." We are not told why our society has this task. In sex education, values are not presented as such. They are assumed and preached. Sex education favors homosexual "intimacy," masturbation, and sex divorced from emotion. It is healthy. That's what the teacher says.

Chapter Seven
Exorcising the Spirit of the Age

1. *A Time for Anger: The Myth of Neutrality* (Westchester, Ill.: Crossway Books, 1982), p. 77. Italics in original.

2. Rousas J. Rushdoony, *The Politics of Guilt and Pity* (Thoburn Press, 1978), sec. III, "The Politics of Money," p. 205:

> Debt rests on covetousness, a desire to possess what our neighbor has, even though we lack his means. As a result of covetousness, the slave desires to possess a home, car, furnishings, and clothing which he sees the wealthy possessing, and his means of securing these things is *debt*. . . .
>
> The covetous man or nation goes into debt to gain added power, purchasing power, prestige, resources, and other forms of visible might. The result is indeed an increase of power, but it is short-term power purchased at the price of long-term disaster. . . . The eventual outcome of a debt-economy, for men and nations, is bankruptcy.
>
> The short-term power, however, is impressive.

3. See J. Brian Benestad, *The Pursuit of a Just Social Order* (Washington, D.C.: Ethics and Public Policy Center, 1982), p. 97.

4. Bishop Leroy T. Matthiesen, in a speech at a peace convention titled, "I Didn't Know the Gun Was Loaded," text dated November 25, 1981. The bishop stated: "We must say: No more, we will throw off the slavery of the nuclear bomb. We will abolish it forever. We will be slaves to fear no more. [And a page later:] . . . peace is possible because we yearn for it." Notice: *Yearning* for something is not praying for it; also, it will be a human act—abolishing the nuclear bomb—that will free us from being "slaves to fear."

5. See J. Robert Nelson, "The Divided Mind of Protestant Christians," in Thomas Hilgers, Dennis Horan, and David Mall, eds., *New Perspectives on Human Abortion* (Aletheia Books, University Publications of America,

Inc., 1981), pp. 387-404. This excellent anthology, dealing with the medical, legal, and social/philosophical sides of the abortion issue, is available from Sun Life, Traxton, Va. 24174.

6. Daniel Dolesh, et al., U.S. Catholic Conference, 1981; devastatingly critiqued in Randy Engel, "A Critique of the USCC Sex Education Guidelines," (St. Paul, Minn.: The Wanderer Press, 1981), and by Henry V. Sattler, in *Laywitness,* November 1981, p. 5 (222 North Ave., Box S, New Rochelle, N. Y. 10801).

7. Sattler, just cited, states: "Though sin is mentioned . . . it is nowhere defined. Sin is made equivalent to 'mistake,' 'imperfection,' 'misuse of ability,' 'immature self-centeredness,' 'dehumanization,' 'violation of our relationship with God and others,' 'manipulation or domination of the weak.' It would almost seem that to the authors sin and finiteness of the individual were equivalent. Nowhere does the concept of guilt or culpability appear. Nowhere in the text is any specific kind of act denominated as sinful. No action is described as one which might violate the will of God. . . ." (The Ten Commandments are not listed, nor does 'Thou shalt not commit adultery' appear in the text.)

8. Randy Engel, p. 48.

9. Ibid., quoting Dom Huber Van Zeller, *The Inner Search* (New York: Sheed & Ward, 1957), p. 4.

10. Francis A. Schaeffer, *A Christian Manifesto* (Westchester, Ill.: Crossway Books, 1981), pp. 46-47, italics added.

11. Ibid.

12. I realize that the Arkansas "creation-science" law recently struck down by a Federal Court was not an ideal method of dealing with evolution in the schools, and that its spokesmen sometimes do the Creationist position a disservice in their rhetoric. But it remains an anomaly that the students hear, largely, only one viewpoint. For in 1968, in *Epperson v. Arkansas,* 393 U.S. 97, a tenth-grade teacher convinced the Supreme Court that an Arkansas statute which prohibited the teaching of evolution violated her First Amendment rights.

13. See L.R. Buzzard and Samuel Ericsson, "Texts, Curriculum, and Parents—Clashing Values," chap. 11 of *The Battle for Religious Liberty* (David C. Cook and Co., 1982), p. 93. This book is available from The Christian Legal Society, Oak Park, Ill.

14. Some forms of "rock" are clearly harmful. See David A. Noebel, *The Legacy of John Lennon* (Thomas Nelson, 1982); and David Kotzebue, *The Rock That Doesn't Roll* (APCO Publishing, 1982), both available from Summit Ministries, Box 207, Manitou Springs, Colo. 80829.

15. It took the U.S. Supreme Court to open up the University of Missouri to voluntary meetings of Christians! See *Widmar v. Vincent,* 102 S. Ct. 269 (1981).

16. See Liz Jeffries and Rick Edmonds, "Abortion," an Appendix in Franky Schaeffer, *A Time for Anger* (Crossways, 1982), pp. 155-87, reprinted from the *Philadelphia Inquirer,* August 1, 1981.

17. In April of 1983, as the guest of a client, I was quartered in one of the finest hotels in New York City. While randomly flipping the station dial on my room T.V. set at 8:00 PM, the "pay movie" channel was showing "coming attractions" of a pornographic movie available for viewing later that evening. Once again, as the serpent showed in Eden, elegant surroundings are no proof against aggressive vice.

18. Just as private schools save the taxpayers' money by reducing the number of children the state must pay for in public schools, so private families caring for their older members reduce the cost of state-provided old people's homes. They are far more humane, too, since the old people receive a love the professional social worker simply cannot give.

    Like the "individual retirement account" (IRA), which permits the taxpayer to reduce his taxable income by (generally) $2,000 if he sets this amount aside in a retirement fund, we could have a similar fund for one's *parents'* retirement, with, as incentive, some reduction of one's own taxes.

Index

Also from Servant Publications

What Is Secular Humanism?
Why Humanism Became Secular and
How It Is Changing Our World
By James Hitchcock

Secular humanism, a body of ideas antagonistic to Christianity, influences our schools, courts, and now even our churches. James Hitchcock, the renowned historian, examines the origins of this ideology and offers a Christian response to the secular humanist agenda. Illustrated, $6.95

The Zero People
Edited by Jeff Hensley

An up-to-date, in-depth, and authoritative treatment of abortion, infanticide, and euthanasia by 25 distinguished authors, social critics, and pro-life leaders. Authors include Dr. C. Everett Koop, Malcolm Muggeridge, George F. Will, Michael Novak, John Powell, and John T. Noonan. Includes color photographs, $7.95

The Christian Mind
How Should a Christian Think?
By Harry Blamires

An acclaimed study of the distinctive Christian intellect by a student and friend of C.S. Lewis. $4.95